G000291747

solar hot water

choosing, fitting and using a system

Lee Rose

LILI

Disclaimer

The authors, publishers, and participating organisations are not responsible for the use or misuse, conclusions drawn or results obtained from any information contained within this book. The information and illustrations are meant as guidance to one or more methods, products and systems that are or have been known to be used. The reader chooses to act upon this information entirely at their own risk and no guarantee of any kind is given as to the outcome of their actions.

All pictures are for illustration only and the products illustrated may differ from those supplied by LILI or any other organisation listed.

Published in February 2012 by

Low-Impact Living Initiative
Redfield Community,
Winslow, Bucks, MK18 3LZ, UK
+44 (0)1296 714184

lili@lowimpact.org
www.lowimpact.org

Copyright © 2012 Lee Rose

ISBN: 978-0-9549171-9-7

Editor: Elaine Koster
Photos: Lee Rose
Illustrations: Lee Rose
Design and Layout: Commercial Campaigns Ltd

Printed in Great Britain by:
Lightning Source UK Ltd, Milton Keynes

contents

illustrations

about the author

For as long as he can remember Lee Rose has always been interested in technical things. As a boy he would spend endless hours making complex models – cars, buildings, bridges, trains, helicopters. He has also had a passion for the natural world and remembers many long summer days spent climbing trees, cycling miles of dirt tracks and country lanes, and wildlife watching along river banks.

Most of his early working life had little to do with technical or environmental things, and then he started a job maintaining buildings, which, after a few years, somehow led him to plumbing college.

Around that time, a pilot scheme was set up by the National Energy Foundation introducing self-build solar hot water systems, based on a successful Austrian model and run in cooperation with LILI and various district councils. Lee volunteered to help with this initiative and soon became known as the 'plumber/installer', helping with many of the installations in Norfolk, where he lives.

Following that he started Norfolk Solar, a small company advising about, designing, installing and maintaining solar water-heating systems with a strong environmental and educational focus.

Since then he has also written books and training manuals and run training courses on the subject for the Council of Registered Gas Installers (CORGI), the BroadSol project, LOGIC Certification and, of course, LILI.

He continues to teach solar hot water courses for members of the public at LILI locations throughout the UK, and for plumbing and heating professionals at the Centre for Alternative Technology.

He holds a City and Guilds qualification in plumbing, and a number of other qualifications in unvented hot water systems, water regulations, energy efficiency, domestic electrical installations, management of health and safety, heat pumps, biomass heating systems, access equipment and photovoltaic systems.

Like many concerned individuals, Lee likes to think he is doing his bit for the natural world; he has been a strict vegetarian for more years than he can remember, monitors his personal (and professional) carbon footprint, and tries to support certain organisations that are doing terrific work to preserve this planet and the diversity of its inhabitants. He eats food grown in his own garden, heats rooms with wood from his own woodland, and, perhaps not surprisingly, generates hot water and electricity from solar power!

introduction

solar hot water: choosing, fitting and using a system is designed to inform and educate on the application of solar-heated water systems and is particularly applicable to domestic dwellings in the UK, although many of the principles described are widely adopted throughout the developed world.

The book does not intend to offer comprehensive guidance on UK regulations surrounding the specification, design, installation and maintenance of solar hot water equipment, and further guidance on this should be sought from the respective agencies and organisations, some of which feature in *resources*, see page 263.

Readers outside the UK should contact the relevant governing body or information service in their country of residence for guidance on relevant regulations.

The information contained in this book comes essentially from a combination of sources including my experiences and involvement in consulting, training and installation work, field trials, technical research, and conversations with friends and colleagues in the solar thermal industry in the UK and around the world.

Naturally, every book is written from a certain point of view and this book is no exception. New products appear all the time and with them come new ideas and new information, and just occasionally this information changes what we believe to be current good practice.

I'd like to take the opportunity here to point out that, from my own personal environmental perspective, any solar thermal equipment that reliably offsets significantly more carbon dioxide (CO_2) than was generated by its manufacture and installation is good solar equipment.

Clearly, some products will do the job better or worse than others, and other considerations, including economic and aesthetic, may also be important, but that's up to you. Where I've expressed an opinion, it's based on my own experiences under certain conditions and doesn't suggest in any way that the outcome will be exactly the same for you.

This book has only been possible thanks to the contributions large or small, formally or just as a chat in a tea break, from Chris Laughton, Phil Hunt, Ben Phillips, Griff Thomas, Mark Krull, Jacek Paluch, Mark Smith, Peter Murphy, all the courses and engineering staff at CAT in Machynlleth, Dave Darby, Dave Hunter, Iain Calderwood, Nick Davies, David Matthews, and all of the wonderfully interesting people that shared their views during and after LILI solar hot water courses over the years.

the need for energy

In 2009, the estimated worldwide population was 6.8 billion. The United Nations predicts that this figure will be around 9 billion by the year 2050, and much of this growth will come from developing countries such as China and India.

Both China and India are experiencing rapid economic growth and this growth requires huge amounts of energy, much of which comes from energy generated by burning fossil fuels.

Whilst developing countries continue to grow, the developed nations are not standing still. In the UK, greenhouse gas emissions from energy consumption in homes between 1990 and 1999 increased by over 6% and by 2009 fell back equating to a 3% reduction compared to 1990 (Office for National Statistics). This is thought to be the result of a combination of energy efficiency measures in the home and a lower consumption due to a contracting economy.

the need for renewable energy

Life on our planet relies on a balance of temperatures. This balance has been maintained naturally throughout our planet's history by the greenhouse effect; a layer of gases in the atmosphere which allows light energy from the sun to heat up the earth's surface and prevents some of that heat from escaping back out to space, thus maintaining a relatively stable temperature.

One of the main constituents of the earth's protective gas layer is carbon dioxide (CO_2), and it is widely accepted that CO_2 levels in the atmosphere have increased alarmingly since the industrial revolution (spanning the 18th and early 19th century).

In just the past 100 years, atmospheric CO_2 concentration has increased by around 25% and this increase corresponds to the increase in burning of fossil fuels.

An increase in atmospheric CO_2 means an increase in the ability of the earth's protective gas layer to retain heat, which may at first seem like an attractive proposition to some people hoping for a more tropical climate. However, destabilisation of the earth's temperature could result in us experiencing:

- more frequent and severe flooding, particularly in low-lying UK areas such as East Anglia, land surrounding the Thames river and other major rivers close to highly populated cities.
- less summer rainfall causing more water shortages.
- a disruption of the natural ecosystem, affecting the population of certain species and those other species that rely on them for food.
- the spread of infectious diseases into geographical areas not previously affected, such as malaria.
- the potential loss of natural warm sea currents and weather patterns such as the Gulf Stream, which is responsible for keeping the west of Europe warmer than other countries of a similar latitude. Ironically, global climate change could actually make the UK a colder place!

The International Energy Agency, see *resources* (page 263), predicts that if worldwide energy generation continues without the benefit of cleaner technologies, then the amount of energy required to satisfy worldwide growth will lead to a doubling of greenhouse gases by the year 2030.

Add to this the estimated known reserves of oil and natural gas (see page 18) and there is a very strong case for localised renewable energy generation.

why solar energy?

Solar energy is by far the most abundant energy resource available on earth and is the source of other renewable forms of energy such as:

- wind energy, which is generated by global wind patterns created from the heating and cooling of the earth and sea by the sun.
- hydropower, which harnesses energy in water falling from altitude. For example, sea water evaporated by the sun forms rain clouds which precipitate onto mountains, the water runs into reservoirs and powers hydro turbines in dams.

- ground source heat from the constant solar radiation falling on the earth and collected using a heat pump.
- biomass fuel, which is the use of crops such as willow for burning, requiring solar energy (through photosynthesis) for crop growth.

World energy consumption is predicted to grow, despite energy efficiency initiatives and energy-saving innovations. Fossil fuel is unlikely to provide a total solution:
- of all the fossil fuels, the largest remaining known reserves are of coal but it is also the most air-polluting fossil fuel. Reserves are estimated at 150 to 200 years supply.
- known oil reserves are estimated to last another 40 to 50 years, though this includes non-conventional reserves which are harder and more expensive to extract.
- natural gas reserves are predicted to run out around 2075 at current consumption rates. However, annual gas consumption is also predicted to rise whilst extraction is set to peak around 2015, after which gas prices are likely to soar.
- known uranium reserves are a fraction of the known gas reserves and there are concerns about the disposal of depleted uranium fuel, security in the face of terrorism and potential damage from nuclear reactor leaks.

By comparison, the solar energy resource is 10,000 times greater than the world's current energy demand, and 160 times greater than the known combined fossil and nuclear fuel reserves. When all the fossil and nuclear fuel reserves have gone, the solar reserve will last for more than a billion years!

In a typical UK home, most of the energy consumed is in the form of heat energy supplying heating and hot water systems, rather than electrical energy for lights and appliances.

The three main types of solar energy gathered for domestic and commercial purposes are;
- solar photovoltaic, also known as PV; the generation of electricity by collecting light through semi-conductor cells made from silicon. Typical collector efficiency is 5 to 15% and collector life span is 15 to 35 years.
- passive solar gain; the passive collection of solar energy by materials, such as granite slabs which are dense and possess a high thermal mass, built into walls and floors so that the stored heat energy can be released over a period of time, usually without the aid of mechanical or hydraulic equipment.
- (active) solar thermal such as solar hot water systems; capturing light

energy for conversion to and subsequent use as heat energy. This technology is far more widespread in the developed world than PV, due mainly to the simplicity of its construction and operation, and comparatively low cost. Collector efficiencies are typically 40 to 60% and should last for 15 to 50 years.

Solar thermal technology for domestic hot water use is the focus of this book.

Harnessing solar thermal energy for use by mankind is not a new concept. In 212 BC Archimedes is said to have employed mirrors to focus the sun's rays in order to burn invading Roman ships during the siege of Syracuse.

In the 1880s a French engineer, Charles Tellier began work on a solar experiment to capture solar thermal energy and convert fluid to steam for powering a mechanical water pump. The solar collectors developed in this experiment were believed to be the early flat plate solar collectors, similar in concept to the 'solar panels' seen on many rooftops today. He went on to use them to heat water in his house.

It's rather unfortunate that many of the pioneers of solar thermal systems lived and worked during the years of the industrial revolution, the period of history which began our reliance on the burning of fossil fuels. This poor timing led to a fifty year slow down in the further development of solar thermal technology.

Since then, solar thermal energy components have undergone significant performance improvements and design modifications. Technical innovations such as highly selective surfaces, highly transparent glazing and improved heat retention methods have allowed solar thermal technology to provide good levels of performance in regions of the world that receive relatively low concentrations of solar radiation. For example, some Scandinavian countries now have an established domestic solar thermal industry despite parts of the region receiving only 40% of the solar radiation experienced in the Mediterranean.

The UK has been slower to move forward with solar thermal technology, due in part to its historical reliance on North Sea fossil fuel reserves, and a lack of political will to first acknowledge, and then address the effects of global climate change – until the Rio earth summit of 1992 and the implementation of the Kyoto protocol in early 2005.

More recently, in 2006, a report estimating the impact of climate change was presented to the UK government. It was compiled by Sir Nicholas Stern, a former chief economist of the World Bank. It has been the widespread view of world economists in recent history that tackling global climate change is too expensive.

The Stern report has gone a significant way towards publicly presenting the economic case to the UK and the wider world for taking rapid positive action to curb climate change, and is considered by some to have the potential to remove the last major reason for doing nothing or not enough.

Compared to other nations such as Israel, which has had a law demanding all new homes have a solar hot water system for more than 30 years, the UK has only recently started to establish the necessary regulations and reduce the unnecessary barriers required to push solar hot water systems into 'mainstream' construction.

Political will is now shifting as the UK has moved from a position of net gas export to net import (via undersea pipelines such as the UK-Belgium interconnector which joins Britain to a trans-European pipeline from Siberia) and wholesale gas prices continue to rise (leaping over 90% at the end of 2005). Add to this the recent rise in annual average oil prices, the increasing focus of government on securing stable energy supplies and the decline in UK coal production and it appears that the UK's interest in domestic solar thermal technology is set to move rapidly in the right direction at last.

Solar thermal systems also benefit from a number of advantages over other renewable/sustainable energy technologies:
- the physical requirements of the installation site are less critical making solar a more flexible choice. Hydropower, for example, requires a local or diverted source of flowing water and wind power requires minimum and constant wind speeds often incompatible with the air turbulence occurring in built-up areas.
- once installed, there are little or no transport demands on the supply of the system's fuel. Lorries do not have to travel back and forth carrying wood chips, pellets or logs as for biomass boilers.
- the technology is typically uncomplicated in design and is therefore often more DIY friendly, more reliable and requires less initial investment.
- solar thermal equipment is less visually obtrusive than other technologies (such as wind turbines) making the technology more acceptable to a wider audience.

- there is no localised noise output or emissions of smoke.
- it is considered by many governments and organisations to be the first choice for small-scale, on-site (as opposed to a centralised power station) renewable energy generation.

why solar hot water?

Solar thermal systems have the potential to capture and deliver heat energy for both hot water and room heating purposes. However, the energy demand for hot water in homes is much more compatible with the solar energy available than energy used to heat rooms.

Although solar energy systems are very good, there are certain things that really should be done before spending money on this technology.

The first thing to do is look at where your house is losing energy; this is fuel that you've already bought and paid for, burnt and released its carbon emissions.

Heat escaping from walls, floors, roofs, windows, doors, unused chimneys and various little gaps can be closed with better insulation, draught strips, and other energy saving solutions.

It may not be as technically appealing, but a thick layer of insulation can save more money and CO_2 emissions than solar energy.

Once you've stopped the heat from getting out, you should find that you don't need to burn as much fuel to get the heat you need, and then you can look at ways to cut your consumption further.

Top tips include:
- turn down your heating and hot water thermostats a degree or two.
- don't let hot water taps or showers run needlessly or at full bore; lowering hot water consumption can also lower the amount of fuel needed to heat it.
- where your heating and hot water system has old and inefficient controls, consider upgrading them to controls which allow more accurate time and temperature control of fuel consumed to heat rooms and water, and consider more advanced weather-compensating controls that adjust fuel consumption down even further according to the outside air temperature.
- insulate hot water cylinders and pipes as much as possible – but take care to avoid covering any electrical fittings.

what is a solar hot water system?

energy flow

Energy input for a solar hot water system takes the form of light energy. This solar radiation must convert to thermal energy in order to provide hot water. This involves processing energy in the following way:

energy capture

Light energy from the sun (solar radiation) is the system's energy source. The amount of light available and the percentage of that energy captured will form the starting point in the energy chain leading to hot water consumption.

energy conversion

This occurs when captured light energy converts to heat and takes place inside a solar collector.

energy transfer

Solar radiation converted to heat must be moved from the point of capture to a temporary storage location.

energy storage

The temporary location where solar-derived heat is allowed to accumulate before consumption occurs. Depending on design, energy may first have to pass from one fluid to another via a heat exchange device.

energy conservation

Conserving the solar-derived heat at all points along the chain until consumption occurs.

energy consumption

Demand for hot water from users.

the objective of a solar hot water system

A well balanced and properly operated domestic solar hot water system in the UK should be capable of contributing 30 to 60% of a household's annual hot water (and more in certain circumstances).

The energy to heat this water is measured in kilowatt hours and, for the majority of homes, the annual energy content of this hot water would be somewhere between 1600 and 3200 kilowatt hours.

Much of the solar contribution will fall between April and October as this offers the best UK solar radiation levels.

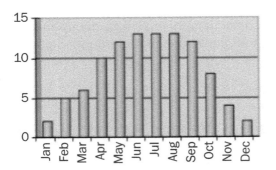

☐ % of Total Solar Contribution

fig 1: annual solar contribution distribution

A reduction in the amount of fossil fuel consumed to heat water will lower carbon dioxide emissions. The amount of CO_2 saved would depend on the fossil fuel being displaced. The CO_2 emissions in kilograms for fossil fuels can vary but UK figures for 2010 were around:

Fuel type	CO_2 per kilowatt hour of energy
Natural gas	0.19 kilograms
Bottled gas	0.22 kilograms
Heating Oil	0.25 kilograms
Coal	0.32 kilograms
Electricity	0.52 kilograms
Wood	0.03 kilograms

This of course has another benefit; the annual fossil fuel costs are lower. The saving will depend on the current and future purchase price of the type of fossil fuel being displaced, but also on other factors that determine just how much solar energy can be harnessed.

It's worth noting that there's a difference between the amount of energy delivered by a solar thermal system and the amount of fossil fuel energy it will displace. This is because some of the thermal energy generated by burning fossil fuel in a boiler will be lost before it can heat water. These heat losses occur in the boiler and other hot water system components and they can make a huge difference to the amount of fossil fuel that is required.

Example: A domestic boiler in a typical space heating and hot water system that is burning natural gas to generate heat may be only 70% efficient. That means, for every 1 kilowatt hour of energy in natural gas, 0.7 kilowatt hours of heat energy can be extracted for practical use.

Where a domestic boiler is burning gas for hot water alone (such as during warm summer months), then the boiler system efficiency may drop to just 35%. That means, in order to add 1 kilowatt hour of heat energy to a hot water cylinder, the equivalent of around 3 kilowatt hours of natural gas is burned.

These figures would be better for domestic houses using condensing boilers or properties with electric heating and hot water.

Taking the old and inefficient non-condensing gas system boiler figures shown above and assuming a solar thermal system could deliver for example 1200 kilowatt hours, the estimated saving in fossil fuel consumption might look like this:

1200 kilowatt hours of solar contribution, 50% (600 kilowatt hours) delivered during months when the gas system boiler is providing hot water only, and 50% (600 kilowatt hours) delivered during months when the gas system boiler is providing space heating and hot water.

For the gas system boiler to deliver 600 kilowatt hours of thermal energy for hot water at low efficiency (35%), 1714 kilowatt hours of gas must be burned.

For the gas system boiler to deliver 600 kilowatt hours of thermal energy for hot water at higher efficiency (70%), 857 kilowatt hours of gas must be burned.

So, the amount of gas-derived energy 1200 kilowatt hours of solar energy would displace in this example is 1714 + 857 = 2571 kilowatt hours.

Note: Try not to confuse boiler-only efficiency with the efficiency of the whole boiler heating and hot water system. Boiler efficiency figures are stated by manufacturers but don't always include losses from the system components (without these components, the resultant heat can't be put to practical use, for example to move thermal energy to hot water in a storage vessel).

basic system layout

A system typically consists of the following elements:

solar collectors

These harness light energy from the sun and convert it to heat energy. The internal surface designed to capture energy is known as an Absorber.

heat transfer medium

This is the fluid used to carry heat energy around the system.

transmission pipes

Provide the route for the heat transfer medium to move between solar collectors and the storage vessel.

storage vessel

A hot water cylinder is commonly used for the accumulation and storage of solar-derived heat energy for use later by the building's occupants.

heat exchanger

If the heat transfer medium contains antifreeze to protect the system against frost, a heat exchanger must be used to safely transfer energy from the collector to the hot water produced from the taps; it can be a coil within a storage vessel or an external heat exchanger.

circulation method

This is the means of moving the collected energy around the transmission pipes; it can be thermosiphon gravity circulation though typically uses a pump.

controller

This is operated by light or temperature sensors for efficient controlling of a circulation pump (where present) to maximise heat gain.

safety devices

These protect the system from damage caused by high pressure or high temperature, and ensure the safe supply of collected energy to hot water outlets.

how it works

The exact components of a system will depend on what the system is designed to supply (for example a swimming pool or domestic hot water) and the method chosen to achieve this.

Here is a simplified drawing of a solar thermal system as found in many of the developed countries of the world.

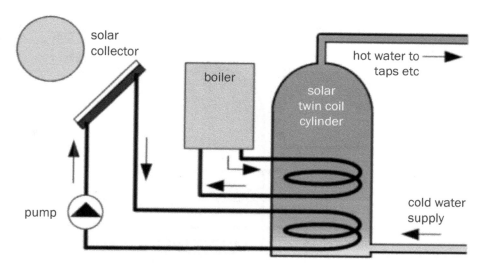

fig 2: solar thermal system

The system has a solar collector and a storage vessel - in this case a hot water cylinder with separate internal heat exchangers for solar and a backup boiler. There are transmission pipes connecting the collector and storage vessel, which will transport heat using a fluid known as the heat transfer medium.

As the solar collector is positioned above the level of the storage vessel, the heat transfer medium must be forced to circulate using a pump.

Fig 3 shows a simple solar thermal system that uses gravity circulation or thermosiphon, and is commonplace in developing nations and regions with good sunny weather.

This choice of system may be due to an absence of electricity required to operate a circulating pump, but may also be a result of the system's simplicity and ability to integrate well with the building practices of the region.

The system operates because a circulation from the point of heat generation (solar collection) to the storage vessel is created because the lower density of hot fluids means they rise above cold fluids.

This is why the solar collector in fig 3 is below the level of the storage vessel.

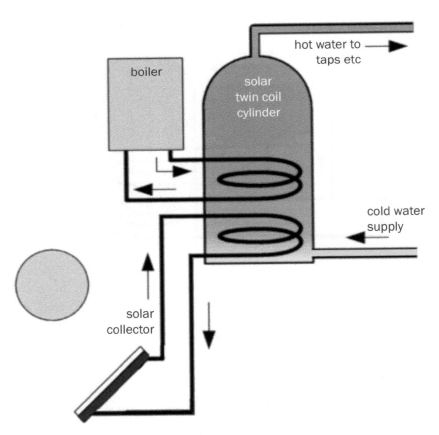

fig 3: thermosiphon solar thermal system

When the sun rises, direct and/or diffuse light begins to strike the absorber surface of the solar collector and causes it to heat up. This heat conducts through the absorber and into fluid-carrying pipes inside the collector.

The heat in this fluid causes circulation – either by natural buoyancy of heat attempting to travel upwards, or by an electronic temperature-measuring device activating a circulating pump.

The circulating fluid (heat transfer medium) carries its heat to a heat exchanger (shown in figs 2 and 3 as a coil in the lower half of the storage vessel), where its heat is given off to the body of cooler water surrounding it.

The heat transfer medium then returns to the solar collector for further heating.

If there is insufficient solar energy to fully heat the water in the storage vessel, a backup boiler or electric water heater is switched on. It's that simple!

key considerations

Achieving a healthy reduction in CO_2 emissions and a reduction in fuel bills is easy enough, but these should be done in a way that is both reliable and safe.

The following issues have the potential to cause harm to either the solar thermal equipment or its users, and should receive careful consideration from the outset.

bacterial growth

The main concern is Legionella, a widespread bacteria living in water, soil and sediments which is not considered a serious risk to health in its natural levels of concentration. It is considered a health risk where conditions allow the bacteria to grow, and where a means of the bacteria entering the deep lung exists.

A suitable means of entering the deep lung could be a bathroom shower, producing a fine spray mist from which the water-borne bacteria can be inhaled by the user.

Such showers form part of many domestic hot water systems and so the issue is not exclusive to solar hot water systems. However, due to variable sun conditions, and therefore variable heat contribution from a solar thermal system, without proper consideration the bacteria may have a greater opportunity to grow more quickly.

Legionella remains dormant below around 20°C. Between 20-50°C, the bacteria can multiply, with peak growth occurring around 38-40°C. Above 50°C, sterilisation occurs within hours or minutes and above 60°C within minutes or seconds.

Legionella favours stagnant water, such as the water found within hot and cold water storage vessels, particularly where stored volumes of water are high and demand for water from users is low.

This essentially points to the need for a backup heat source, to boost the temperature of stored solar-preheated water to ensure sterilisation where insufficient solar radiation has been harnessed to do the job alone, and the correct sizing of stored water vessels to balance water demand against bacterial control.

Legionella also likes nutrients upon which to feed. These might be from a range of sources but would include foreign objects that have entered the water system, such as dead insects or vermin falling into uncovered water storage vessels (most commonly a cold water vessel supplying a hot water vessel).

This means storage vessels should have lids, and shouldn't have open connections that could allow foreign objects to enter the water supply.

More information is available from the UK Health and Safety Executive, see *resources* page 263.

water-soluble minerals

This is mainly calcium bicarbonates dissolved in water supplies, otherwise known as limescale.

The amount of mineral deposits in a water supply will vary from region to region (even opposite ends of the same village) and this information can often be easily obtained from public sources such as the local water provider. In some areas the concentration of calcium is high enough to require action and prevent long term damage to a domestic hot water system.

Limescale deposits left unchecked are quite capable of reducing the operating efficiency of heat exchangers and heating elements resulting in higher fuel bills. Where calcium-rich water is passed directly through a solar collector, the damage can be quick and irreversible.

It can also clog up water supply pipes and outlets; showers become an unpleasant dribble and running a bath seems to take forever.

fig 4: main picture – a hot water cylinder cut open to show years of limescale build-up. Inset picture – a cross-section of a scaled-up pipe leading to dramatically reduced water flow rate

Where concentration is above 200 parts per million, a water softening or conditioning device should be installed.

Simple water testing kits for assessing the concentration of calcium bicarbonates are available from plumbing supplies merchants.

high temperature and pressure

A modern solar hot water system is easily capable of generating liquid temperatures of 100 °C under certain conditions and in certain components.

Where the liquid is part of a sealed system and under pressure, it has the potential to remain in liquid form well above 100°C (see table, fig 5) and beyond this, liquid undergoes a phase change and rapidly expands (in the case of water to 1600 times its original volume) to form vapour.

Pressure	Boiling point (degrees C)	
	Water only	Antifreeze mix up to 50% (ratio dependent)
at Atmospheric	100	+ approx 2 to 6
+1 bar	120	+ approx 2 to 6
+2 bar	133	+ approx 2 to 6
+3 bar	143	+ approx 2 to 6
+4 bar	152	+ approx 2 to 6
+5 bar	159	+ approx 2 to 6
+6 bar	165	+ approx 2 to 6

fig 5: varying boiling points

In order to ensure many years of trouble-free solar energy contribution, any materials that are likely to come into contact with such high temperatures would of course need to reliably withstand these conditions.

High temperature surfaces and fluids should be installed and delivered in such a way that they are unlikely to harm anybody, and pressurised fluid-carrying components should have an adequate quantity and type of safety devices.

freezing

The UK experiences enough periods of sub-zero temperature to require the protection of some components from frost damage.

A host of methods are adopted by manufacturers to achieve this and the use of antifreeze is by far the most popular way of protecting solar collectors. UK weather statistics including minimum temperatures and number of air frost days for a given location can be obtained from the Meteorological Office, see *resources* page 263.

solar collectors

Commonly referred to as solar panels, these are the flat glass panels seen on many rooftops, but they may also take the form of a series of glass tubes connected to a manifold.

fig 6: flat glass solar panel

fig 7: glass tube solar panel

The purpose of a solar collector is to capture solar energy for heating water. Light striking the solar collector passes through the glazing and is received by the absorber.

The purpose of the absorber is to receive solar energy and conduct the resultant heat along its mass to a heat transfer medium.

The purpose of the insulating parts of a solar collector is to prevent captured heat from being lost through the collector casing.

Different collectors perform this function with different degrees of success and it is important to understand that the solar collector is just one of a series of equally essential components.

how big is a solar collector?

The size of a solar collector can be defined in four ways:
1. the physical width, length and depth
2. the gross surface area; a footprint of the entire collector measured in square metres
3. the absorber surface area; a footprint of the absorbing surface alone, ignoring any surrounding area occupied by insulation, air gaps or structural elements of the collector
4. the aperture surface area; a footprint of the surface area that light can pass through to reach the absorber. This footprint includes any mirrors used to reflect light

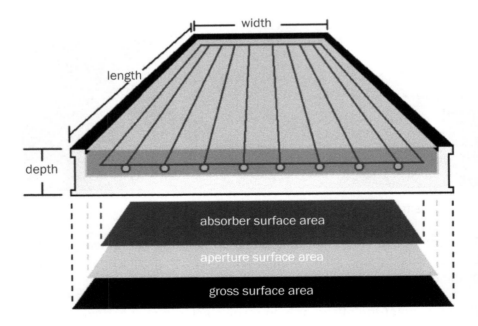

fig 8: sizing a solar collector

evacuated tube solar collector

This type of collector consists of one or more sets of glass tubes containing a flat strip or cylindrical absorber, connected to a well-insulated pipe manifold.

Evacuated tubes employ a vacuum layer between the absorber surface and the outer glazing to minimise heat loss. The glass tubes may have a single or double glass wall construction. The absorber is held inside the glass tube and may be a direct flow absorber or an indirect 'heat pipe' assembly (see following section).

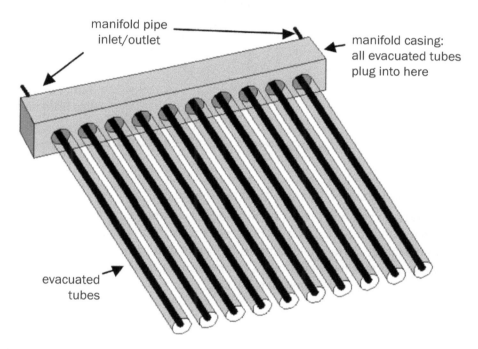

manifold pipe inlet/outlet

manifold casing: all evacuated tubes plug into here

evacuated tubes

fig 9: evacuated tube solar collector

types of glass tube construction

single glass wall or 'glass-to-metal' evacuated tubes

These glass tubes have a single layer of glass sealed at the ends by a metal cap. The entire cavity of the tube contains a vacuum which is maintained by the glass-to-metal seal. The transmission of light through a layer of glass improves as the thickness and number of layers of glass is reduced.

This means that a single glass wall tube will typically have very good optical performance when compared to a double wall construction.

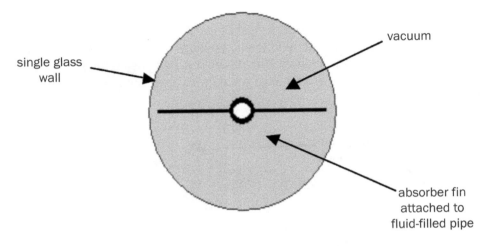

fig 10: cross-section of a single-walled, evacuated glass tube

double walled glass or 'Sydney' evacuated tubes

Developed as a solution to the potential loss of vacuum experienced in some glass-to-metal tubes (caused by different thermal expansion rates of the glass and metal surfaces leading to failure of the vacuum seal), Sydney tubes are in effect two glass tubes connected together at the ends using the same glass they are constructed from.

The vacuum is retained between the two layers of glass and heat transfer elements are placed in a vacuum-free (normal atmosphere) cavity inside the inner glass tube. The inner glass tube is usually coated with the collector's absorbing surface and a curved metal heat transfer fin passes heat energy from this glass surface to fluid-filled pipes inside the vacuum-free cavity.

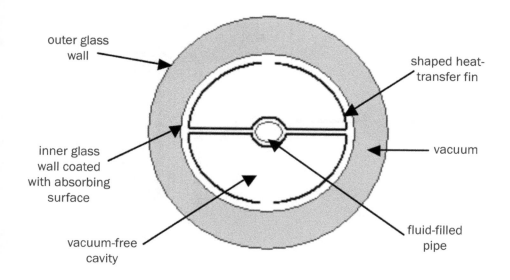

outer glass wall

shaped heat-transfer fin

inner glass wall coated with absorbing surface

vacuum

vacuum-free cavity

fluid-filled pipe

fig 11: cross-section of a double-walled, evacuated glass tube

types of heat transfer assembly in an evacuated tube

In addition to differences in glass tube construction, the process of transferring heat from the absorbing surface to a heat transfer medium will also vary. There are currently several designs and the most popular are described below.

direct flow evacuated tubes

The fluid circulating through the collector's manifold pipe is passed directly through a pipe assembly within each glass tube and back to the manifold pipe. Direct flow tubes are available in conjunction with single or double wall glass tube construction. This type of tube array is capable of achieving temperatures exceeding 250°C in UK sunny conditions.

In the UK and other regions that experience frost, direct flow tubes will normally require an antifreeze mixture as the heat transfer medium.

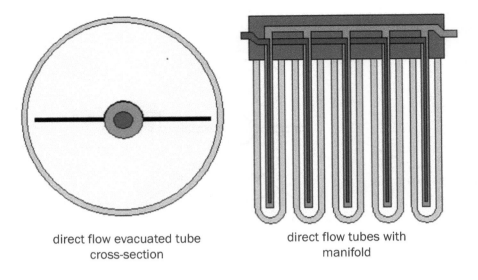

direct flow evacuated tube
cross-section

direct flow tubes with
manifold

fig 12: direct flow evacuated tubes

heat pipe tubes

A heat pipe tube is a sealed copper pipe with a 'plug-in' condensing tip at the manifold end, containing a separate fluid designed to vaporise at low temperature. As the absorber converts light to heat energy, the sealed fluid is vaporised and rises up the heat pipe to the condensing tip. The solar heat transfer medium, passing the condensing tip in the manifold pipe, absorbs heat via conduction and the heat pipe vapour condenses back into its fluid form.

The separate fluid travels back down within the heat pipe, where the process can be repeated. Heat pipes require a minimum angle of installation to operate as they rely on the principle of heat rising. This minimum angle varies slightly from manufacturer to manufacturer but is generally in the region of 30°.

Heat pipes are often available in single or double glass wall evacuated tubes.

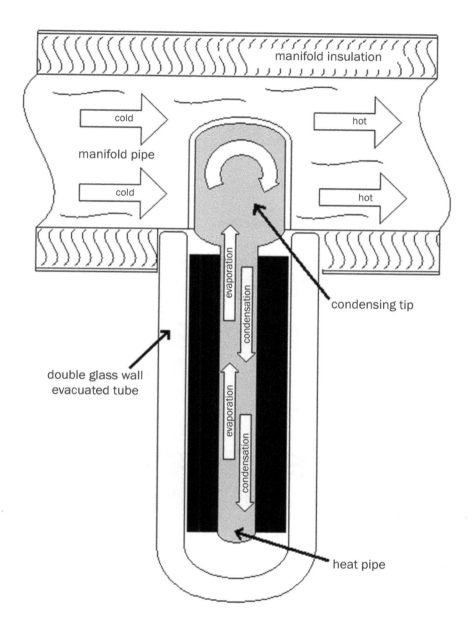

fig 13: heat pipe tubes cross-section

flat plate glazed solar collectors

This has been the most commonly installed type of solar collector for the past 30 years.

home-made flat plate collectors

These consist of a weather-resistant casing normally made from materials that are of limited durability, primarily due to the cost and availability of suitable materials.

Absorbers range from salvaged and recycled radiators to an assembly of copper pipes soldered to metal fins and painted black (for further details about making your own solar panels, see *building a solar collector*, page 235).

modern factory-made flat plate collectors

A weatherproof casing, usually of pressed or extruded aluminium alloy contains a plate absorber attached to a series of small-diameter pipes. There is normally a thick layer of insulation to the back and sides of the absorber and single glazing to the front.

fig 14: commercially produced flat plate collector

Flat plate collectors use insulation material to minimise heat loss, which is less effective than a vacuum. The surface area-to-energy output of flat plate collectors is usually lower than that of evacuated tubes, but they are often cheaper to buy, and preferred in visually sensitive locations.

Modern flat plate collectors are generally considered to be a very robust design due mainly to their simplicity and long history of reliability.

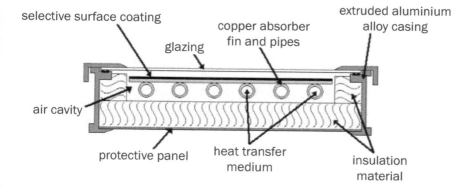

fig 15: cross-section of a typical modern, flat-plate solar collector

The pipes carrying the heat transfer medium that are attached to the collector's absorber fins can be arranged in a variety of ways, and some absorber and pipe combinations are best suited to particular solar thermal systems.

harp or headers and risers design

A formation of horizontal and vertical pipes, the top and bottom horizontal pipes are larger diameter - typically 18 to 22mm - and are called **headers**. The vertical connecting pipes are often 8 to 10mm in diameter and are directly attached to the absorber fins. These are called **riser** pipes.

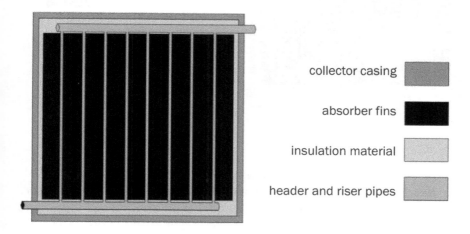

fig 16: harp or header and risers design

In this design, the heat transfer medium enters the collector through the bottom *header* pipe, then passes into each *riser* pipe. As the fluid reaches the top connection of each *riser* pipe (by now it has absorbed heat from the attached fins), it remixes into the top *header* pipe and leaves the collector.

As there are many possible routes for the fluid to travel through the collector pipes, the fluid has very little frictional resistance. This makes the *harp or headers and risers* collector design very suitable for solar thermal systems using thermosiphon circulation.

Note also that this collector design forces the fluid to take an equidistant path from entry to exit; this is important as it prevents the heat transfer medium from taking a 'short cut' which could allow inefficient hot and cold spots to develop within the collector.

Absorber materials are copper pipes, copper or aluminium fins.

A variation of the *harp* absorber is the *split harp* absorber.

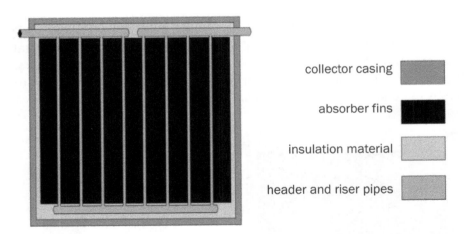

collector casing

absorber fins

insulation material

header and riser pipes

fig 17: split harp absorber

In this design, the heat transfer medium enters the collector at one side of the top *header* pipe and is forced downwards through each connected *riser* pipe. The fluid remixes in the bottom *header* pipe and passes into *riser* pipes in the second half of the absorber, travelling upwards where it remixes in the top *header* pipe and exits the collector on the opposite side.

As there are fewer possible routes for the fluid to travel through the collector pipes (compared to a standard *harp* design), the fluid has more frictional resistance. This means fewer *split harp* collectors can be connected in series, and more pump energy may be required.

Also, the path of the heat transfer medium through the absorber means that this design is unsuitable for use in solar thermal systems using thermosiphon circulation.

Absorber materials are copper pipes, copper or aluminium fins.

serpentine design

As the name suggests, a single pipe takes a *serpentine* path through the collector, typically 10 to 15mm diameter.

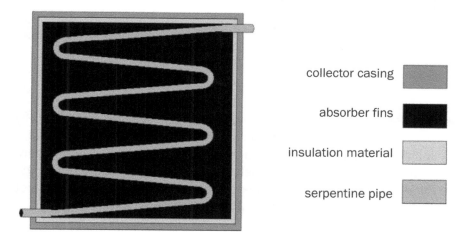

fig 18: serpentine design

Having only a single pipe, the heat transfer medium is forced through the absorber 'in series'. This can result in a greater temperature difference between the top and bottom of the absorber depending on the rate of flow. It also means that the heat transfer medium has more frictional resistance as it travels through the collector.

As fig 18 shows, *serpentine* collectors often have a minimum fall angle on their pipes; this allows them to be used in *drainback* solar thermal systems, where fluid is required to reliably exit the collector by gravity when the circulating pump is deactivated.

However, there are some **serpentine** absorbers which are only suitable for fully-filled, pressurised solar thermal systems.

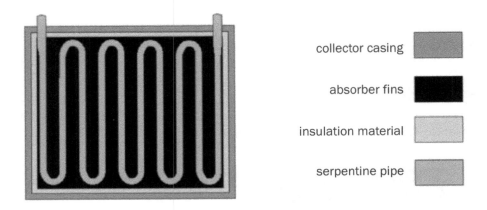

collector casing	
absorber fins	
insulation material	
serpentine pipe	

fig 19: serpentine absorber for pressurised solar thermal system

In this design, the single pipe meanders across the absorber vertically which, if used in conjunction with a vented solar primary circuit would result in the build up of air in the highest parts of the collector and may stop flow. It would also prevent the heat transfer medium from draining out of the collector in the case of a **drainback** system, which could result in frost damage if the heat transfer medium did not include an antifreeze.

Absorber materials are copper pipes, copper or aluminium fins.

cushion absorber

Also known as a 'pillow' or 'fully-flooded' absorber, this design allows the heat transfer medium to flow across the entire absorber surface area.

During manufacture, two sheets of absorber material (often stainless steel) are welded together at the seams and in spots evenly placed over the entire surface area.

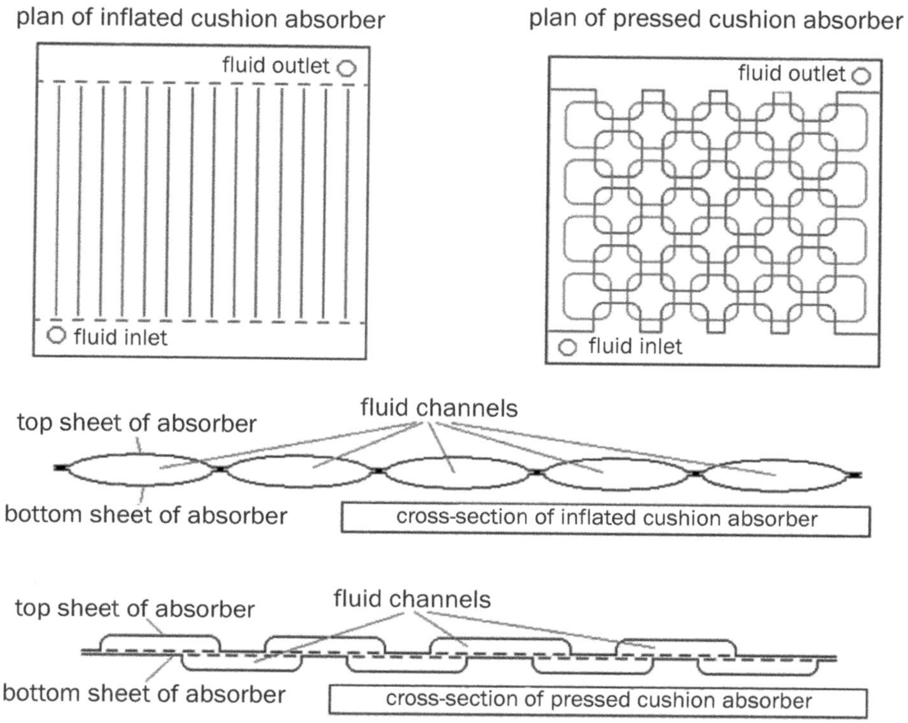

plan of inflated cushion absorber
plan of pressed cushion absorber

fluid outlet ○

fluid inlet ○

fluid outlet ○

fluid inlet ○

top sheet of absorber

fluid channels

bottom sheet of absorber

cross-section of inflated cushion absorber

top sheet of absorber

fluid channels

bottom sheet of absorber

cross-section of pressed cushion absorber

fig 20: cushion absorbers

These sheets may be pressed with specially designed channels prior to welding or may be flat; in this case the flat sheets are welded together and compressed air is then forced into the absorber separating the sheets to form channels.

The heat transfer medium flows into the absorber from one corner and travels through the channels, exiting the absorber at the opposite corner.

Flat plate collectors using **cushion** absorbers tend to cost more than **serpentine** or **harp** absorbers which reflects the higher costs of manufacturing.

All models are suitable for use in pressurised solar thermal systems and some are suitable for use in **drainback** systems.

Absorber materials are all stainless steel.

flat plate collector glazings

Modern flat plate solar collectors are available with a range of glazing formats.

The purpose of the glazing is to maximise the amount of light reaching the absorbing surface whilst minimising the heat lost from the collector, and protecting the internal elements of the collector from rain, snow and dirt.

Current glazing formats available include:

single pane toughened glass

By far the most common glazing format and well proven, this is typically made using glass with a low iron content (also known as 'solar glass'), which is believed to slightly increase the amount of light able to pass through.

The thickness of the glass affects the light transmission (thinner glazing = more light transmission). Single pane toughened glass is normally around 3-4mm thick (depending on the overall surface area).

double pane toughened glass

Offers better heat retention (similar to window double glazing) than single pane, but light energy must travel through two layers of glass, reducing the light energy striking the absorbing surface. This design also dramatically increases the collector's gross weight as the glass often accounts for most of the weight of a collector.

single sheet acrylic

Not a common glazing for collectors, acrylic glazing has better light transmission properties than glass and is significantly lighter, but cannot withstand heat as well. Therefore, acrylic glazing is manufactured with a curve to help prevent sagging caused by high temperatures from the absorber.

Acrylic glazing may become brittle and prone to cracking with old age and exposure and will not match the predicted lifespan of glass.

single sheet twin-wall or triple-wall polycarbonate

Also not a common glazing format, twin-wall polycarbonate has two very thin layers (double glazed) combined into a single sheet, with an air gap between the layers. It is a very lightweight glazing format with very good light transmission properties but may be prone to sagging under high temperature. Many small supports are normally used to 'prop up' the polycarbonate glazing, keeping it away from the high temperature absorber. Polycarbonate also has a shorter lifespan than glass.

Twin-wall or triple-wall polycarbonate is elsewhere commonly used for making roofs on UPVC conservatories.

flexible membranes
Extremely lightweight and thin, flexible membranes have very good light transmission properties.

They are used in different ways by collector manufacturers; some favour two layers of membrane, and others favour an exterior single pane of glass with a secondary membrane layer.

In order to limit sagging, membranes are stretched tightly over the glazing frame of the collector.

Flexible membranes have a much shorter lifespan than glass and in certain circumstances (such as birds landing on or pecking the membrane), can be easily damaged beyond repair.

insulation materials in glazed solar collectors

Certain aspects of the construction of both flat plate and evacuated tube collectors are the same. For example, although individual evacuated tubes use a vacuum to retain heat, the manifold must use similar physical insulation as that found in flat plate collectors.

As you would expect, all of these materials have good insulating properties though some may deteriorate in certain conditions, reducing performance.

Insulation materials used include:

mineral wool
Probably the most widely used insulation in solar collectors today, mineral wool can be manufactured to fit any cavity; it can be made into loosely-bound and highly-flexible blankets or compressed into a more rigid product. It is light in weight and has an extremely long lifespan. The insulating performance of mineral wool will drop if it is allowed to absorb water.

synthetic rigid foam

There are many variants of synthetic polymer rigid foams available for use as heat insulators. Some variants that have been used as thermal insulation in solar collectors are polyisocyanurate, phenolic, polyurethane and polystyrene foams though some are not suitable for use within solar collectors due mainly to their inability to withstand high temperatures, resulting in materials melting or giving off fumes or sticky residues.

Synthetic rigid foams are sometimes used in conjunction with a thin layer of mineral wool, where the mineral wool is used to protect the synthetic material from high temperatures.

selective surfaces

The development of selective coatings for solar collectors provided a major boost to operating efficiency.

Essentially, a selective surface is designed to be very good at allowing energy of a certain wavelength (mostly ultraviolet and short wave visible light) to pass into the surface whilst being very bad at allowing energy of a different wavelength (long wave heat energy) to pass out of the surface.

There are several different brands of selective surface used to coat absorbers within solar collectors and the base materials used in their manufacture can vary.

As a result, the performance of selective surfaces will differ somewhat though there is unlikely to be a big enough variation to influence the choice of collector.

The base materials used and the apparent colour of the sky has the effect of altering the appearance of a selective surface.

Some surfaces will appear deep blue or purple on clear days and blue/grey on cloudy days, whilst others appear black regardless of the weather.

In addition, some brands of selective surface have recently been developed to coordinate with the surrounding roof covering; these new colour-matched surfaces are currently very limited in availability and using them means a compromise is made between aesthetics and performance.

It is worth mentioning that the absorbers within some solar collectors use non-selective coatings. This is almost always matt black paint and they would not perform as well without it although this underperformance may not necessarily be a significant concern if, for example, the collector is required to achieve lower temperatures, such as for swimming pool heating.

pipe connections for solar collectors

Manufacturers of solar collectors must contest with a long list of design considerations, one of which is how to connect individual solar collectors together, and another is how to pass fluid-carrying pipes from outside the roof to the void beneath (such as a loft void or room space).

This is important as poor detailing can lead to rain passing through the roof, and increase the time taken for their product to be installed, making it potentially less attractive to their customers.

Unsurprisingly, manufacturers have differing views on the ideal design and solutions include:

side entry pipe connections

Connecting pipes are fabricated on one or more sides of each collector, allowing for extra collectors to be easily attached. They are used on flat plate and evacuated tube collectors. This design requires a separate weather tight means of passing fluid pipes through the roof covering.

fig 21: side entry pipe connections

top entry pipe connections

All pipes containing fluid pass through the top edge of the collector casing allowing discreet routing of pipes. They are used on flat plate and evacuated tube collectors. This design requires a separate weather tight means of passing pipes through the roof covering.

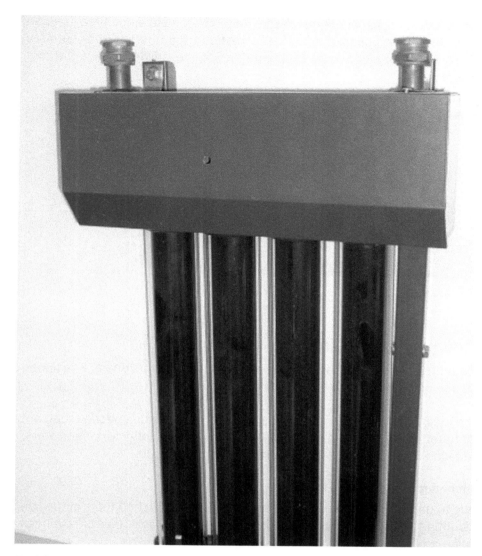

fig 22: top entry pipe connections

rear entry connections

Predominantly found on flat plate collectors, the pipe connections pass through the rear of the collector and directly through the roof covering. This design is particularly useful for flat plate collectors that are integrated into the roof using a special flashing kit, avoiding any visible pipe connections on the roof and removing the need for a separate means of weatherproofing for pipes passing through the roof covering.

A less appealing aspect of this design (in terms of installation time) is when more than one collector must be connected together as this requires interconnecting pipes to be fabricated inside the building below the roof covering.

fig 23: rear entry connections

mounting options for solar collectors

Mounting kits are generally supplied with solar collectors and are designed for use on a limited range of installation surfaces.

The majority of solar collectors are installed on an existing pitched roof, but manufacturers offer optional mounting kits where collectors need to be installed on a vertical (wall) or horizontal (floor) surface.

pitched roof mounting kits

Due to the wide variation in roof coverings used on pitched roofs in the UK, mounting kits are usually designed to fit a limited range of tiles or coverings and are product specific.

On-roof mounting kits are designed to install the solar collectors above the existing roof tiles or covering; tiles may be removed during installation but on completion all tiles are returned to the roof.

In-roof mounting kits allow the solar collectors to be integrated into the roof covering; a section of roof tiles or covering is permanently removed and the collector is installed in this area using a weatherproof flashing kit.

Examples of mounting options include:

stainless or galvanised steel flexible straps

These are normally only supplied with certain brands or models of evacuated tube collectors and are suitable for installation on most clay and concrete interlocking roof tiles, and both natural and reconstituted slates.

Due to the difficulty of drilling, these straps are supplied with predrilled holes to allow for adjustment to different roof tiles.

One end of each strap is fixed to structural timber (such as roof rafters) using coach screws and the other end is fixed to part of the frame upon which the collector is mounted. They are suitable for on-roof mounting of collectors.

fig 24: flexible steel strap

alloy semi-rigid straps

Historically favoured by UK solar collector manufacturers for their versatility, alloy straps are usually only supplied with certain brands or models of UK made flat plate collectors.

Made from type 6063 aluminium alloy, these straps can be easily formed using a hammer but are sufficiently rigid and strong to maintain the desired shape.

Due to the thickness of the straps, it is sometimes necessary, depending on the type of roof tiles, to cut a channel in the back of tiles installed directly over straps so that all tiles may sit properly on the roof and maintain a good weatherproof covering.

One end of each strap is fixed to structural timber using coach screws and the other end is fixed either to a mounting frame or directly to the collector casing. They are suitable for on-roof mounting of collectors.

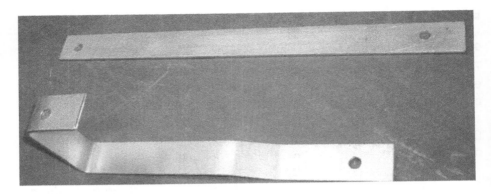

fig 25: alloy semi-rigid straps

hook type brackets

Cast from aluminium alloy or pressed from heavy-gauge galvanised or stainless steel, this is often part of the standard mounting system supplied by many European solar collector manufacturers – both flat plate and evacuated tube.

One end of the bracket is hooked over the top edge of a roof tile and the wooden tile batten directly beneath. The other end of the bracket is bolted to a frame onto which the solar collector is mounted.

Given that the system essentially relies on the strength of wooden tile battens to carry the extra weight from collectors and frame, there is often a minimum requirement for these wooden battens specified by the manufacturer (such as rot-free timber with no knots, a cross-section of at least 25 x 75mm and strong, screw-in timber fixings).

The heavy gauge of metal used means that each bracket cannot be re-shaped during installation so bracket designers have devised clever ways to adjust the brackets to fit a wide range of roof tiles, using a range of washers (spacers) and a selection of predrilled holes.

An unfortunate effect (in terms of time) of the bracket's thickness is the need to cut a channel in the back of each roof tile resting on a bracket, to ensure a weather tight roof.

The brackets are suitable for use on most clay and concrete interlocking roof tiles and individual designs may allow a wider application.

Another variant of the hook type bracket uses the same hook shape for fixing to the collector or collector mounting frame, but the fixing to the roof rafter is via a footplate with predrilled holes, allowing the bracket to be positioned according to the available flattened sections or channels of the roof tiles, see fig 26. They are suitable for on-roof mounting of collectors.

fig 26: hook type bracket with footplate

profile rails

Constructed from aluminium alloy or galvanised steel, profile rails may be supplied as part of a mounting system including other brackets or straps, or may be the predominant component for mounting solar collectors.

The profile will vary according to manufacturer but may be as simple as an 'L' profile with no predrilled holes or an elaborate extrusion with special channels that use high speed fixings for a rapid collector installation.

Supplied by some evacuated tube and flat plate collector manufacturers throughout the world, profile rails are mainly designed for on-roof installation on a pitched roof but some products can also be used for vertical or horizontal mounting (if the collector design allows this).

Often suitable for use with clay and concrete interlocking roof tiles, slates and various sheet roofing materials.

fig 27: profile rails

integrated roof mounting kits

As the name suggests, a section of the roof tiles is permanently removed and the solar collector is installed in their place.

Where the edges of the collector meet the existing roof tiles, a pre-fabricated set of weather tight flashings are installed. Each section of flashing is designed to fit a specified edge of the collector; upper, sides and lower, so as to ensure that water running down the roof is correctly diverted over or around the solar collector without the roof leaking!

Any gaps in the roof tiles not filled by the collector flashings must be filled with roof tiles cut to size and shape.

They are suitable for use on most types of tiles and slates but not generally designed for use with sheet roofing.

Integrated roof mounting kits are only supplied with appropriate flat plate solar collectors for in-roof mounting onto a pitched roof. A minimum roof angle will usually be specified by the manufacturer, and is not normally less than 27°.

vertical or horizontal mounting kits

As the majority of homes are built with pitched roofs this is the least popular type of mounting.

Where a solar collector needs to be wall or floor mounted, it is almost always desirable to adjust the angle of the solar collector. The advantage of doing this is that the performance of each square metre of surface area of the collector is optimised, therefore saving the cost of extra or bigger collectors.

The drawbacks are:
- the collector stands proud of the surface it is attached to; this may not necessarily be unattractive but planning permission may be needed
- the collector is more prone to the lifting effect of strong winds and so extra measures may be needed to stop the collector from being blown away

fig 28: collector with horizontal mounting

A-frame mounting kits

These mountings consist of a series of rails and bars bolted together to form triangular cross-sections which are linked by diagonal bars (for bracing) and horizontal rails (for mounting the collector). Some designs have a ballast tray bolted to the bottom.

A-frames can be made from aluminium alloy or steel (painted mild, galvanised, or stainless) and attached to the surface by:

- mechanical fixings such as bolts or coach screws where fitted to walls or floors that can be drilled without affecting their weather tightness
- weights such as concrete blocks, gravel or bricks (which are loaded into frames with built-in ballast trays)
- the fixing surface must be in good structural condition to prevent wind forces acting on the solar collector from pulling fixings out

wall mounting systems

These are rarely used in the UK as wall mounting systems are normally designed for larger solar installations such as office blocks, where the solar collectors become a part of the building's façade.

Similar in concept to the rails used to mount collectors on a pitched roof but fixed directly to the wall structure, they are often mounted so that the glazing appears perfectly flush with the surrounding wall cladding.

solar collectors for swimming pools

This book seeks to cover solar thermal systems predominantly for supplying domestic hot water and not swimming pool heating. However, here is a brief overview of collectors suitable for swimming pool heating, mainly to show why they are unsuitable for a domestic solar hot water system.

The solar heating of swimming pool water has distinctly different requirements to a solar thermal system for providing domestic hot water.

Swimming pools operate at relatively low temperatures and for this reason, heat losses from solar collectors become less important.

Swimming pools may be outdoors or indoors, and this will partly determine the choice of solar collectors. Indoor swimming pools tend to be used all year round and often the roof covering of the pool house means that the pool doesn't benefit from passive solar heating. In this case, the use of glazed solar collectors as previously described would be a sensible choice.

An outdoor pool can receive a solar contribution in two ways; passive solar heating as the sun falls on the water, and active solar heating from an unglazed solar collector using pool water as the heat transfer medium.

Unglazed solar collectors have no heat-retaining insulation. This is because outdoor swimming pools are normally only used when the ambient air temperature surrounding the pool is comfortably warm and there is not normally an intention to use the pool through the winter months.

This warm ambient air temperature and the relatively low temperature requirements of the pool water (typically around 28°C) allow the unglazed and uninsulated solar collector to operate efficiently without the need to complicate collector design in order to retain heat.

This leads to a collector design that is actually little more than an absorber, with fluid-carrying chambers resembling those of its glazed and insulated relative; often a fully-flooded cushion absorber or harp absorber with many small-diameter risers.

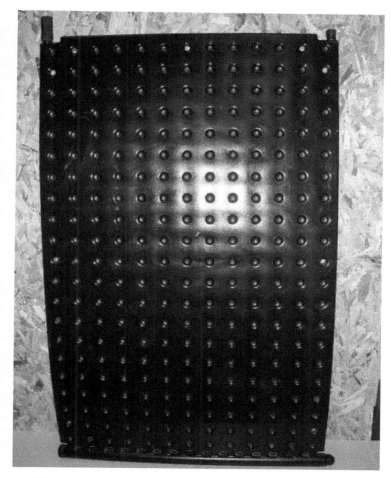

fig 29: unglazed solar collector

The most distinctive characteristic of this type of solar collector is its construction material. Unlike glazed and insulated collectors with absorbers manufactured from copper, aluminium or steel, an unglazed and uninsulated swimming pool collector would almost always be constructed from ultraviolet-light resistant plastic.

This is possible due to the low temperatures during operation, simple design and the need to pass chlorinated pool water through the collector (a source of damage to some metals).

solar collector selection

In order to select a suitable solar collector, you should consider:
- **space:** how much space is available on the roof (or wherever you have chosen)? The size and shape of space you have will determine the range of collector types you can choose from for the volume of hot water you need.
- **mountings:** does the chosen collector have a suitable method of roof mounting for the type of roof? Will you need special tools for mounting?
- **collector construction:** how durable is the collector and how often might you need to gain access to it? (For example, aluminium casings would tend to last longer than wood.)
- **collector weight:** what is the weight of each collector when dry and what method will be used for lifting it onto the roof? Is it practical?
- **system type:** does the system design require a certain type of collector? (For example, drainback system.)
- **wind resistance (exposed locations):** which collector designs have lower wind resistance or are special mountings needed?

collector testing and performance

The factory-made solar collectors previously described are increasingly required to undergo independent testing to ensure consistent build quality and performance, and provide reassurance to consumers.

In the European Union, this testing is undertaken by approved test facilities to a harmonised standard known as BS EN12975. The standard comprises elements to assess collector durability (part 1) and performance (part 2).

Part 1 features a range of tests including:
- ability to withstand high temperature and long periods in the absence of a heat transfer medium

- temperature shock tests
- resistance to leakage and distortion from internal pressure
- resistance to rain penetration
- resistance to frost damage
- resistance to impact on the collector glazing
- an upward pressure test on the collector glazing
- a downward pressure test on the glazing (simulating snow and wind loads)
- an upward pressure test on the collector mountings (simulating wind uplift)

Following collector testing, a BS EN12975-1 report is generated and will illustrate all elements where a pass or fail mark has been awarded, and will detail any observations made.

There are similar testing regimes in Australia and the United States of America, but you should be aware that not all of the elements of these tests are compulsory to award a pass certificate and some product manufacturers in these countries opt out of certain tests.

Part 2 of BS EN12975 is a performance assessment for which there is no pass or fail.

Collectors are placed in a predetermined system installation, with a storage vessel (the energy load), and subjected to a minimum amount of solar irradiance for a specified time period.

Whilst the system installation, energy load and irradiance received may bear little resemblance to a real-life installation, the test results do provide a fair means of comparing relative collector performance.

However, it should be remembered that test parameters are not real-life conditions, and BS EN12975-2 test results should not be seen as a guarantee of collector output under any conditions other than those exactly matching the testing regime.

Key results from Part 2 testing include:
- **zero loss efficiency (eta 0)** This describes the maximum efficiency of a collector when absorber and ambient air temperatures are equal and under a measured amount of irradiance. It defines the highest possible efficiency the collector will achieve.
- **heat loss coefficient (a1) and temperature dependence of heat loss coefficient (a2)** define how collector efficiency drops as the difference

in temperature between absorber and ambient air increases. It should also be stated under a measured amount of irradiance.

- **the efficiency curve** is plotted on a graph with qualifying data stated such as the measured irradiance during testing (in watts per square metre) and the reference area of the collector used (for example, aperture area in square metres). The peak of the curve coincides with a zero value along the X-axis and illustrates the zero loss efficiency of the collector. The curve dips from here to an X-axis value around 0.06 which illustrates the main temperature-difference operating range of a solar collector when heating domestic hot water. The decline of this curve can give a fair indication of comparative collector efficiency.

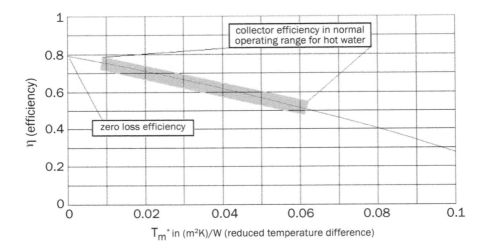

fig 30: collector efficiency curve for G (global irradiance) = 800 W/m² related to the aperture area

In practice, collector performance is linked to system design; a well-balanced system and regular hot water demand (the energy load) will permit solar collectors to absorb more of the available solar irradiance and transport this energy away for heating water.

If the ratio of stored water-to-collector surface area is too small, the collector will spend more operating hours at a higher average temperature, thus reducing its efficiency and gross energy yield, see *system design* chapter, page 125.

CEN keymark for solar collectors

Commonly known as the solar keymark, this is a test of solar collectors according to the BS EN12975 standard described previously, but the main difference is that the testing institution is responsible for personally selecting the individual samples to be tested. This ensures that the solar collectors are an accurate representation of the quality of the product delivered to the end users from the factory production line.

The solar keymark is currently considered the highest pan-european testing standard for solar collectors.

the solar collector array

Where more than one solar collector is needed to deliver the desired energy contribution, collectors must be connected together in an array.

The way in which collectors are arranged can affect their performance and the reliability of the complete system, and an array arrangement should balance these objectives against any site-specific issues to be overcome.

collectors in series

A series connection provides a single path for all heat transfer medium entering the array to travel through all absorbers to the exit point. As the heat transfer medium moves through the absorbers, solar energy is accumulated.

The single route through the array forces the heat transfer medium to spend a longer period of time gathering solar energy or, a greater flow rate is needed to force the heat transfer medium through in less time in order to keep the temperature difference between the first and last absorbers in the array to a minimum (a smaller temperature difference equals better operating efficiency).

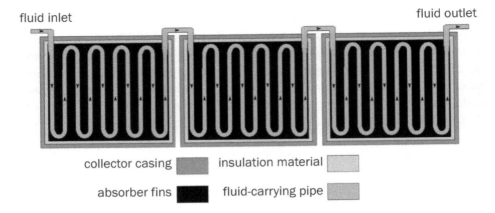

fluid inlet

fluid outlet

collector casing ▮

insulation material ▯

absorber fins ■

fluid-carrying pipe ▯

fig 31: collectors in series connection

collectors in parallel

Collectors connected in parallel provide a variety of paths for the heat transfer medium to pass through the absorbers from entry to exit point. As the heat transfer medium moves through the common manifold pipe, it divides in volume and a portion flows through each of the absorbers until the portions rejoin in a combined pipe leading to the exit point. Solar energy is accumulated through this process, but the temperature difference between the collectors in the array will be less for a given flow rate than those arranged in series.

The operating temperature of a collector and its effect on efficiency is explained previously in this section.

Collectors arranged in parallel have a lower frictional resistance to fluid moving through them than those arranged in series and the route from entry to exit is likely to be shorter. This could mean less power is required from the circulating pump.

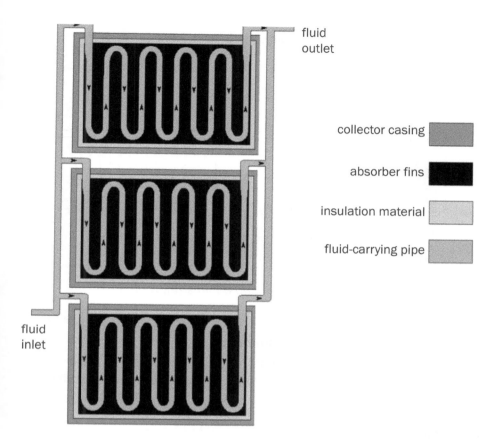

fluid outlet

collector casing

absorber fins

insulation material

fluid-carrying pipe

fluid inlet

fig 32: collectors in parallel connection

array hot spots and short circuits

Hot spots and short circuits can reduce collector efficiency and lead to premature degradation of a glycol-based (antifreeze) heat transfer medium.

As the heat transfer medium will try to follow the shortest path through an array, it is desirable for all possible routes from the common entry point to the common exit point to be equidistant, so as to avoid one or more collectors operating at a higher temperature.

fluid following the shortest route through an array of harp absorbers

fluid passing through the array is forced to follow an equidistant route from inlet to outlet

short circuits where fluid moves quickly

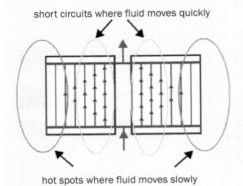
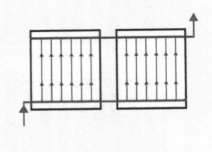

hot spots where fluid moves slowly

fig 33: array hot spots, short circuits and equidistant routes

solar collectors – questions and comments

Here are a few common questions and comments together with some theories and opinions. As with most subjects, they do not constitute the only, definitive answer:

'why choose flat plate collectors when evacuated tube collectors are much more efficient?'

There are a number of issues to consider here and this statement often assumes choice is dictated on the basis of better heat retention by a vacuum:

manufacturing quality and collector efficiency

Poor product design or quality control during manufacturing can affect a collector's ability to allow light to reach the absorber surface, transfer heat from the absorber to the heat transfer medium, and retain heat outside vacuums (such as the heat in an evacuated-tube collector's manifold casing). The fact that it is an evacuated tube collector doesn't automatically make it more efficient than a flat plate collector in all conditions.

absorber to ambient air temperature

In order for heat to be lost from a collector, there needs to be more heat in the absorber than in the surrounding air. The greater this temperature difference, the more potential heat loss there is.

By keeping the absorber to ambient air temperature difference small, less heat can potentially escape. Where heat has escaped from an absorber, using vacuums or physical insulation materials is the next line of defence in retaining heat.

Absorber temperature can be kept relatively low by ensuring that any captured heat is quickly moved out of the collector by a pumped heat transfer medium. Lowering the desired solar-heated-water temperature also helps to maintain a small absorber to ambient air temperature difference. Solar collectors used to heat a swimming pool achieve a much lower average temperature difference than collectors used in a high temperature (above 100°C) industrial heat process.

Ambient air temperature is dictated by local weather conditions, and colder weather makes it harder to maintain a small absorber to ambient air temperature difference whilst capturing useful solar heat.

An example would be a cold but very sunny winter day, and this is one occasion where absorber heat loss could be effectively reduced by a vacuum. Unfortunately, the reduced levels of solar radiation and number of sunshine hours during winter days often means only a small difference in *annual* energy benefit is observed between the collector formats.

snow

In locations where snow is common, it may be an advantage to use a solar collector that allows small amounts of heat to leak out. Snow covering a solar collector will only allow part of the available light to pass through to the absorber beneath. Light that strikes the absorber will convert to heat and as a temperature difference is established, some heat will attempt to escape to the ambient air.

The vacuum in an evacuated tube collector will try to prevent this uncontrolled movement of heat, but in a flat plate collector, some of this heat will move freely to the underside of the collector's glazing surface where it will begin to melt the snow directly above. This in turn removes more snow and allows more light to strike the absorber, increasing the potential solar contribution for the day.

reliability

If a particular evacuated tube collector had a claimed 20% higher efficiency than its flat plate equivalent but its design causes a recurring fault where no heat was generated, the amount of energy it could harness would be lower over the long term. If I had to choose the single most important factor when selecting solar collectors, it would be reliability.

size

An evacuated tube collector will often occupy slightly less space than a flat plate collector, but this difference in size will depend on the exact construction of the evacuated tube collector. Some are made with large gaps between each glass tube and a large mounting frame, whilst others are more compact.

Where roof space is concerned, the total surface area (not active, aperture or absorber surface area) plus any space needed for pipes and brackets is all important.

cost versus environmental benefit

The economic and environmental costs of a particular collector need to be weighed against its energy benefit (the fossil fuel its energy has displaced). As the source of fuel (the sun's rays) costs nothing in monetary terms to buy, provided there is enough space to install the surface area of solar collectors needed to deliver the energy required, their efficiency could be argued to be less important.

If a larger area of one product can deliver the same energy benefit for a lower price, and that collector consumes less energy and resources during its manufacture, then it is better value, for the money and for the environment. This is one of the reasons why flat plate collectors still enjoy popularity.

system design

Some designs require the use of a solar collector which allows the heat transfer medium to move in a particular way. An example would be a *drainback* system, where all of the heat transfer medium must be able to drain freely from pipes within the collector when circulation stops.

Some solar collectors require a system design which allows heat to pass from collectors to hot water taps in a particular way. An example would be a fully-filled system using some models of single glass wall evacuated tube collector.

In this case, generated heat must be removed from the collector to ensure thermal stresses do not break the glass-to-metal seal in each tube, potentially causing a loss of vacuum. This need to keep collectors 'cool' has the effect of increasing stored hot water temperatures to well above 60°C, and in turn may dictate the use of thermostatically controlled hot water outlets to prevent scalding.

installation requirements

The choice of solar collectors suitable for installation into the roof covering is rather limited. Some flat plate collectors are designed to allow such integration but gaps between the glass tubes of an evacuated tube collector generally prohibit this type of installation.

These are just examples of why more than just one solar collector type is available, and should remain so.

'which type of collector is the most reliable; flat plate or evacuated tube?'
It is unfair and inaccurate to say that all flat plate collectors are more reliable than all evacuated tube collectors (or vice versa) because, as with all technologies, there is a wide range of product quality and working experience.

As an industry, we do know much more about the durability of flat plate collector design, simply because we have shared in the evolution of these products for many more decades than the newer evacuated tube technology.

At the moment, we can evaluate collector durability in the following ways:

independent testing

The European Union has established a standard durability testing regime for solar collectors called BS EN12975. This attempts to subject products to a series of accelerated lifecycle tests and the passing of these rigorous tests does offer considerable peace of mind.

user feedback

Learning from the experiences of real users in real situations (rather than laboratory conditions) is increasingly useful and accurate with the passing of time. However, there are few organised mechanisms to impartially gather and publish this information, and the process involves a significant time delay when newer technologies may be replacing those being monitored. In its simplest form, a friend's recommendation makes for limited but nevertheless valuable user feedback.

industry feedback

There are numerous product experts and professionals with excellent hands-on experience who will be prepared to share their honest knowledge regarding a certain product's durability. Unfortunately, there are also those who are happy to distort honest knowledge if it increases sales. This measure of durability is perhaps the least dependable!

It is worth noting that poor system design can allow a perfectly reliable solar collector to make other system components unreliable. A good example of this would be where other components are exposed to working temperatures higher than their design limits. Temperatures between 70°C and 180°C may affect some rubbers and plastics, and above this temperature, soft metal compounds (such as solder) may struggle to remain watertight. This is particularly relevant where collectors capable of temperatures in excess of 230°C are used (most flat plate collectors would be unlikely to reach this temperature in UK conditions).

'if a single glass tube in an evacuated tube collector breaks, it can be replaced easily without switching off the system or draining the heat transfer medium'

Theoretically, this is true to some extent. In practice, it doesn't apply to every evacuated tube collector and can be potentially dangerous work because:

- some models will release pressurised heat transfer medium if a single tube is unplugged
- apart from the risk of handling the broken glass tube (usually at height), by removing a tube you may be exposing very hot metal surfaces (although not always)
- some direct flow models require a minimum amount of free working space in order to slide glass tubes away from the collector, and the roof shape or other obstructions may mean this isn't always possible

If an evacuated glass tube does break it is probably due to:

- a manufacturing defect preventing the glass tube and adjacent metal surfaces from expanding properly, causing the glass to crack. This usually occurs soon after the collector has been installed and so should be covered by the product warranty.
- an impurity in the glass used to make the tube. In this instance, the tube will generally crack soon after it has been exposed to solar radiation and should be covered by the product warranty.

- something heavy is dropped on the glass tube, like a brick. This is very unlikely to happen and so doesn't typically form part of a manufacturer's design criteria.
- a glass tube is broken or damaged during transportation. Subject to good packaging, this isn't the fault of the manufacturer and these things happen.
- a design or installation defect either in the collector or the system as a whole prevents the collector from coping with the combination of high pressure and temperature under certain conditions (typically high solar irradiance and low hot water demand). This only affects a small percentage of evacuated tube collectors but where it does, this may occur every summer or not occur for several years. It does highlight the importance of matching the right products and services from organisations with good knowledge and experience to the estimated operating conditions in the building's hot water system.

It is also worth noting that only a handful of flat plate collector models are manufactured in such a way that the glazing could be readily replaced. However, the glazing in flat plate collectors tends to be thicker (sometimes twice as thick as in evacuated tube collectors).

'heat pipe evacuated tubes are self-limiting'
Self-limiting in terms of the maximum temperature the collector will generate and true to some extent with certain models; check with the product manufacturer.

Due to the evaporation and condensation cycle in heat pipe models, the process of generating very high temperatures (for example, during high solar irradiance and low hot water demand) can be limited.

If evaporation has occurred within the heat pipe but no heat is removed by the heat transfer medium in the collector's manifold pipe, the heat pipe fluid cannot condense and move down into the field of irradiance. Therefore, no further heat can be carried by the evaporated fluid and the heat generation cycle slows down.

Heat trapped in the evaporated fluid does not completely stop heat transfer, as further heat can conduct upwards through the metal walls of the heat pipe but at a much slower rate, hence only partially self-limiting high temperatures.

Some models go a step further by utilising a temperature-sensitive heat transfer device near the heat pipe's condensing tip, which is designed to block evaporating heat above a specific temperature (around 130°C) from moving into the condensing tip.

The purpose of a self-limiting device is to lower the maximum operating temperature of the solar collector and therefore reduce the potentially harmful effects of high temperature on other system components.

'flat plate collectors are quicker and easier to install than evacuated tube collectors'

Due to the wide range of designs, sizes and weights of solar collectors, it would be untrue to say that all models of any one format are quicker and easier to install.

Certainly small size and low weight are useful where a lot of manual handling is involved, but this needs to be balanced against the time savings offered by moving fewer, but larger and heavier collectors.

Practically, it depends on resources and techniques. A team of skilled installers with suitable access and lifting equipment can make light work of a single large and relatively heavy collector, whereas an inexperienced installer with few resources would be likely to appreciate a small, lightweight collector (or a collector that can be moved in pieces).

The moving of sectional or complete collectors is only part of the time- and effort-saving calculation. The installation of mounting brackets and frames, weatherproof flashings, roof tiles and collector pipes should also be considered and there are many clever designs to save time and effort; so if you are the installer, it's a good idea to spend as much time evaluating these as the collector itself.

Both flat plate and evacuated tube collectors include models that are large and heavy or small and light, and even if you aren't contemplating installing the collector yourself, a poor choice could increase the time, complexity and hence price you pay for an installer to complete the job for you.

hot water storage vessels

These are most often referred to in the UK as a hot water cylinder, hot water tank, immersion heater or boiler. Whilst the first two are perfectly reasonable descriptions, its worth being just a little 'picky' about the latter two names;

- an immersion heater is the electrical element that is installed inside a hot water storage vessel and has its electrical heating element immersed in the water, hence the name
- a boiler can rightly be described as a container in which stored water is heated, but in the world of domestic heating the term can be confused with that of the household gas- or oil-fired boiler, which doesn't go by another common name

If you are using this book to help choose somebody to supply or install solar water heating equipment for you, it's never a bad idea for you and the installer or supplier to use the same names for key components – it can only reduce the chances of confusion, conflict or unnecessary expense.

The purpose of a hot water storage vessel is to store water that will be heated at a certain time but not necessarily used until later.

To perform this task efficiently it must be:

- capable of allowing one or more heat energy source to efficiently add heat to the stored water, usually by means of an integrated heat exchanger
- able to retain enough heat energy in the water to satisfy the needs of the user at a later time. To do this the vessel will need to be insulated and hold a sufficient volume of water
- clean and hygienic, to prevent harmful organisms from affecting the health of those using water from the storage vessel

storage vessels and solar energy

Most of the hot water storage vessels currently installed in UK homes were not originally designed to receive solar energy. These existing storage vessels would generally have the following common features:

- one or more immersion heaters to heat stored water by electricity. A second immersion heater is usually configured to take advantage of off-peak cheap rate electricity.

- a single heat exchanger connected to the main water heating appliance such as a gas, oil or solid-fuel boiler. This heat exchanger will have been specifically designed for this purpose.
- a water inlet receiving cold water from a storage tank within the building or directly from the mains water supply.
- a hot water outlet passing heated water into the pipe system that distributes hot water to taps, showers, baths and other appliances.
- a pressure device or outlet. When water is heated it expands, increasing the water pressure. If this pressure is not carefully controlled or allowed to escape, it could split the storage vessel. A pressure device or outlet could be a simple open-ended pipe at a safe location (such as a vent pipe terminating over a cold water storage tank) or a more complex set of valves and thermostatic devices discharging pressure to a pipe terminated safely outside the building (appropriate when the majority of stored water is received into the storage vessel directly from the mains water supply).

This following diagram (fig 34) shows the flow of water and heat through an existing hot water storage vessel (simplified and with pressure device or outlet not shown):

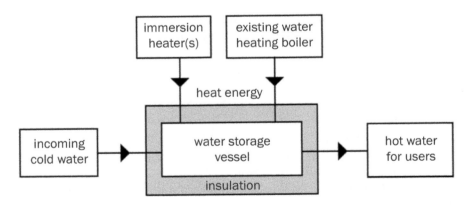

fig 34: existing hot water storage vessel

Fig 35 is a simplified diagram showing the addition of solar energy:

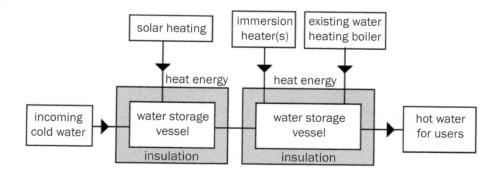

fig 35: solar energy incorporated into an existing system

Although fig 35 shows the solar heated energy being exchanged into a physically separate storage vessel, it could also be a part of the same storage vessel connected to the existing water heaters.

solar heat exchangers

Many solar thermal systems for hot water (indirect systems – for an explanation of direct and indirect systems see page 78) require an additional heat exchanger dedicated to delivering solar energy. This may take the form of a coil within the storage vessel or a plate-type exchanger outside the vessel.

fig 36: samples of special finned tubing used to make internal solar heat exchange coils

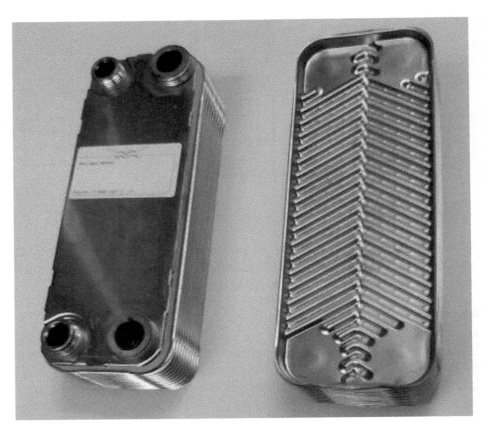

fig 37: plate-type heat exchanger

The main differences are:
- external plate heat exchangers can be replaced independently of the storage vessel
- external plate heat exchangers generally require an extra circulating pump (additional to any pump that may be required in the solar thermal system) in order to transfer heat to the stored water

As internal-coil-type heat exchangers represent by far the largest percentage of solar thermal system designs in Britain, this type is shown where appropriate in the following diagrams.

separate solar storage vessel

As the name suggests, solar energy is delivered to a separate storage vessel and allowed to preheat this water before being passed into another storage vessel where any shortfall in heat can be added by the existing water heaters. Water then passes from this storage vessel to the hot taps, showers etc. This is also known as a solar preheat cylinder.

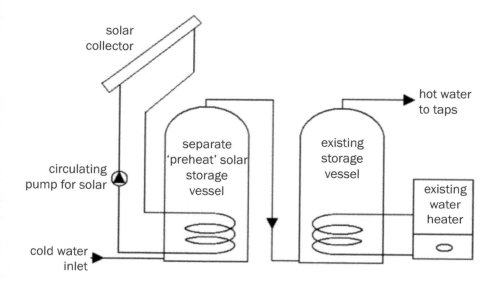

fig 38: solar preheat cylinder incorporated into an existing system

combined solar storage vessel

In this design, solar energy still occupies a dedicated volume of water but within the same storage vessel as the existing water heaters.

As warm water is heated, it becomes buoyant and so rises upwards. The combined solar storage vessel uses this principle to ensure that solar energy has a volume of water at the very bottom of the storage vessel that cannot be heated by existing water heaters positioned higher up, therefore ensuring that free and environmentally friendly solar energy is not displaced by expensive and polluting fossil fuel energy.

This system is also known as a solar twin-coil cylinder and should not be confused with a 'combination' cylinder which, in the UK describes a cylinder with a built-in cold water storage cistern at the top (see the vented cylinder section, page 80).

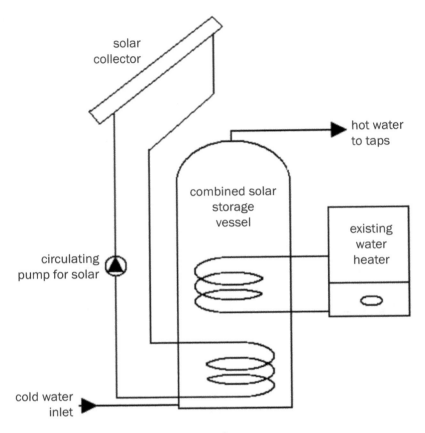

fig 39: combined solar storage vessel

solar connected to an existing storage vessel

Given that most existing storage vessels in UK homes were not originally designed to accept solar energy, this method doesn't have the benefit of a volume of water that can only be heated by solar.

The existing boiler is often connected to a heat exchange coil in the very bottom of the storage vessel and solar energy is added by either:

- **direct connections;** the solar heat transfer medium enters the storage vessel near the top and leaves near the bottom. As stored hot water and heat transfer medium are the same liquid, antifreeze cannot be used.
- **indirect means;** via a special heat exchanger in the top of the storage vessel. This heat exchanger replaces the electric immersion heater. Separation of the stored hot water allows antifreeze to be used in the solar heat transfer medium.

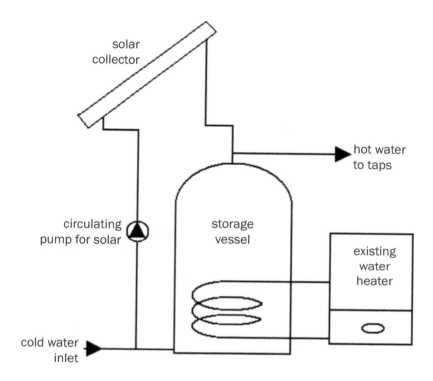

fig 40: existing storage vessel with direct solar connections

existing storage vessel with indirect solar heat exchanger replacing immersion heater

When solar energy is connected directly to an existing hot water storage vessel, great care should be taken to prevent the existing water heaters from being allowed to heat stored water during the daylight hours. If this were to happen, the existing water heaters could add fossil fuel heat faster than solar and displace the free and environmentally friendly heat energy.

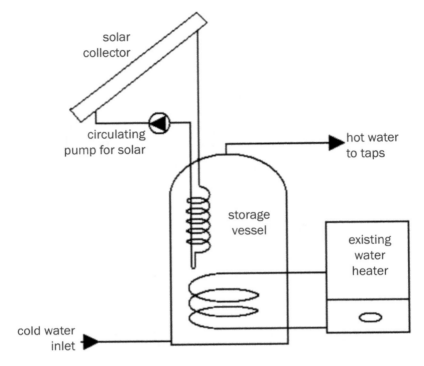

fig 41: existing storage vessel with indirect solar heat exchanger replacing immersion heater

common types of UK solar storage vessel

vented cylinder

This is probably the most common storage vessel, due mainly to the number of existing homes that have a vented hot water system prior to solar technology being installed.

Fig 42 shows a twin-coil solar-vented hot water cylinder. Mains pressure cold water is delivered via a float-operated filling valve to a cold water storage cistern (usually mounted in a roof space). From here, all water to the hot water cylinder and onward to all hot water taps is delivered by gravity alone.

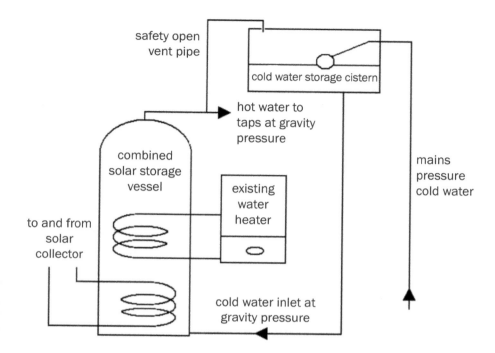

fig 42: twin-coil solar-vented hot water cylinder

As gravity is the source of water pressure for this system, the height of the cold water storage cistern above the hot taps and other outlets is important – a higher cistern will provide greater hot water pressure. For every metre the cold water storage cistern sits above the hot water outlet, a water pressure of 0.1 bar is gained.

Properties of a vented solar storage vessel:
- less expensive than other storage vessel types
- less materials used in manufacture
- simple and reliable
- low operating pressure can equal less hot water consumption
- straightforward installation compared to other storage vessels
- can be manufactured as a separate (preheat) cylinder or combined (twin coil) solar cylinder
- can be manufactured as a vertical or horizontal cylinder (horizontal is not recommended in twin coil solar format)
- when heated, the main body of fluid is allowed to freely expand into the cold water storage cistern above and if overheated, fluid can also exit the cylinder through a permanently open vent pipe

unvented cylinder

This type of cylinder is becoming more popular in the UK as the demand for high-flow showers increases. An unvented hot water storage vessel is designed to receive mains pressure cold water from its source and, once heated, deliver similar good water pressure to hot taps, showers etc. This removes the need for a separate booster pump on a high flow-rate shower.

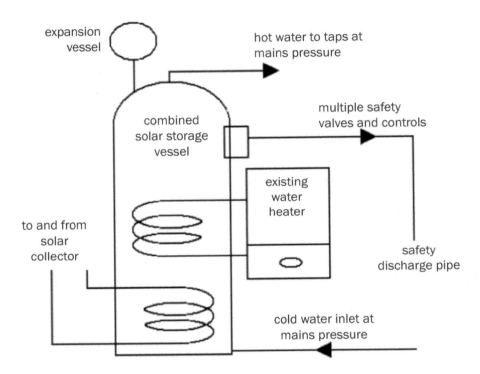

fig 43: unvented cylinder

Properties of an unvented solar storage vessel:
- high flow rates available without booster pumps (where water source allows)
- removes the need for cold water storage cistern
- balanced hot and cold water pressure at outlets
- can be manufactured as a separate (preheat) cylinder or combined (twin coil) solar cylinder
- can be manufactured as a vertical or horizontal cylinder (horizontal is not recommended in twin coil solar format)
- when heated, the main body of fluid is allowed to expand into a dedicated expansion vessel, and if overheated, fluid is discharged by temperature- and pressure-controlled safety valves

- more expensive than vented storage vessels
- more components = more complex
- specially qualified installer required to install safely and legally

thermal store

A departure from conventional hot water storage vessel design, the thermal store reverses the roles of the fluids being stored.

In a conventional storage vessel (such as a vented or unvented cylinder), the bulk fluid being stored is called the secondary fluid. This is the fluid that enters the storage vessel as wholesome (drinking quality) cold water and leaves as wholesome hot water for delivery to taps and other outlets.

The fluid passing through a heat exchange coil from heat sources such as a gas- or oil-fired boiler is called a primary fluid and is not wholesome as it may be mixed with corrosion inhibiting chemicals.

In a thermal store, the bulk fluid being stored is primary fluid and is directly circulated to a gas- or oil-fired boiler. The wholesome cold water is passed through a special heat exchange coil and delivered to taps as wholesome hot water (the secondary fluid).

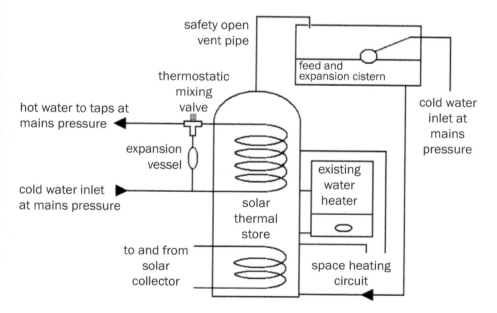

fig 44: thermal store with a separate feed and expansion system

Fig 44 shows a solar thermal store with a separate feed and expansion cistern but this cistern can also be built into the top of the thermal store if required. Please note that the diagram shows connections from the thermal store to a space heating circuit. Thermal stores can be manufactured to supply heat energy from the main body of fluid (primary fluid) to a heating system.

Thermal stores are designed to deliver hot water on demand and must be constantly hot. In contrast to vented or unvented cylinders, an existing water heater connected to a thermal store is not normally time controlled. Instead the thermal store uses temperature controls to switch the water heater on or off as required ensuring the thermal store's main body of water does not fall below 50°C.

The permanently hot state of a thermal store, its ability to activate a fossil fuel water heater during daylight hours and the disrupting effect of pumped circuits on stratification (the layering of water – hottest at the top and coolest at the bottom, see page 85) all have a negative effect on the performance of a solar heating system.

Properties of a solar thermal store:
- high flow rates are available without booster pumps (where water source allows)
- removes the need for cold water storage cistern
- balanced hot and cold water pressure at outlets
- when heated, the main body of fluid is allowed to expand into a dedicated feed and expansion cistern
- when heated, the secondary fluid is allowed to expand into a dedicated expansion vessel
- more expensive than vented storage vessels
- constantly high operating temperatures in the thermal store reduce solar contribution. Larger stores (over 400 litres) and stores with special stratifying devices suffer less from this effect

general principles of solar hot water storage vessels

All of the storage vessels previously described will allow the storage of hot water for a limited period of time, typically less than 72 hours. A modern solar hot water system is designed to provide a home with a significant amount of the hot water required each year.

In the UK much of this contribution will be between the months of April and October, with a much smaller contribution during the winter months.

In an ideal world, we would be able to capture solar energy throughout the summer months (when solar energy is more abundant) and store that energy for use during the winter. Unfortunately, one of the major obstacles to collecting energy in the summer for use in the winter is the lack of a cost-effective vessel that can store heat energy for more than a few days.

It may be technically possible to design a solar thermal system capable of delivering the energy needed to meet 90-100% of annual hot water demand, but this would lead to excess potential energy in the summer in order to meet the demand in winter, would offer poor value for money and generate more carbon dioxide emissions to manufacture the extra equipment needed.

In other words, it would perform well in the context of delivering all of your hot water needs all of the time, but at an unreasonable cost.

In order to get the best out of a storage vessel heated by solar energy, the following factors should be considered:
• stratification
• heat retention
• solar heat exchange
• temperature measurement
• storage vessel volumes and dimensions

stratification

This is the natural layering of water according to its density. As water is heated, it becomes less dense (lighter) and so rises above the cooler water.

Stratification is good for solar thermal systems because a solar collector will work more efficiently if the temperature of fluid that is passed into it is lower than the fluid leaving it.

This fluid is normally supplied via a connection at the lowest point in a storage vessel, ensuring that the fluid temperature is as low as possible.

Stratification is also good for comfort as it ensures that the hottest water is the first to be supplied to the household hot water outlets.

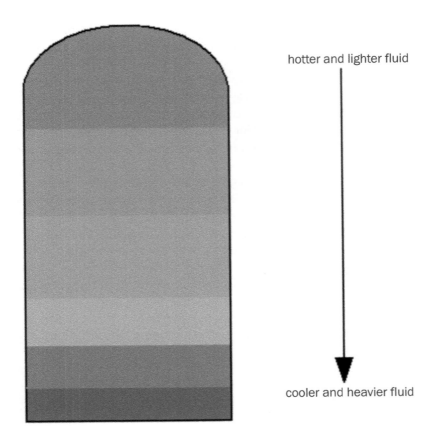

hotter and lighter fluid

cooler and heavier fluid

fig 45: stratification pattern

Stratification can be improved by:
- large storage vessels
- tall and thin storage vessels
- storage vessels with built-in dividers or baffles to limit turbulence

Stratification can be disrupted by:
- short and wide storage vessels
- small storage vessels
- turbulence caused by pumped fluids entering and leaving the storage vessel that are able to mix directly with the stored fluid
- cool fluids pumped into areas of the storage vessel holding hotter fluids

heat retention

All new hot water storage vessels will have some kind of insulation to limit the amount of heat loss. Heat loss occurs when the air temperature surrounding the hot water storage vessel is lower than the water temperature inside the vessel. A cold and draughty location will encourage greater heat loss and require better storage vessel insulation.

Insulation types currently in use include flexible mineral wools and rigid foams. Different insulation materials have slightly different heat retention properties. The thickness of insulation ranges from around 35mm to 100mm. Thicker insulation will benefit all energy sources supplying heat to a storage vessel, not just solar. Also, thicker insulation applied to the hottest parts of a storage vessel (the top) will improve heat retention.

Good application of insulation is essential; fewer gaps in the insulation layer equals less heat loss. A poorly fitting insulation jacket has large gaps which allow greater heat loss and the same applies to gaps around pipe connections to the storage vessel.

solar heat exchange

Storage vessels with an internal heat exchanger that separates wholesome water from the fluid passing through a solar collector are very popular in the UK.

On any given day, a solar thermal system will be operating at constantly varying temperatures. This is mainly due to the varying amount of solar energy striking a collector as the sun rises and sets, and clouds pass overhead. This means that the temperature of fluid passing from the solar collector and into the storage vessel may sometimes only be marginally higher than the wholesome water being stored.

A storage vessel of this type therefore needs a much larger heat exchanger in order to transfer a small amount of heat energy effectively. The surface area of a solar heat exchanger (measured in square metres) is often more than twice that of a heat exchanger connected to a fossil fuel water heater, which delivers heat via a primary fluid at a constantly high temperature.

A system using a storage vessel where the fluid passing through a solar collector is able to mix with the wholesome (secondary) water is commonly known as a 'direct solar hot water system'.

This type of storage vessel transfers heat readily as there is no physical barrier limiting the heat exchange. In addition, because the fluid passing through the solar collector is the same fluid that ultimately leaves the hot water outlets, no antifreeze chemicals may be added. This is beneficial in terms of heat exchange because the heat-carrying capacity of wholesome water is higher than that of water mixed with antifreeze.

temperature measurement

Most solar thermal systems are controlled by comparing the temperature of the fluid in a solar collector with the temperature of fluid in a storage vessel.

Where this is the case, it is important that the temperatures being compared are as accurate as reasonably possible and a solar storage vessel is often manufactured with dedicated pockets which allow temperature sensors to measure secondary water in the centre of the vessel rather than along the side wall.

The absence of these pockets could result in the solar thermal system inappropriately circulating fluid (for example when there is too large or too small a temperature difference between the collector and storage vessel) leading to a drop in system performance.

storage vessel volumes and dimensions

Hot water storage vessels are available in various volumes, heights and diameters. To help get a feel for what size vessel could fit, there is a cylinder volumes/dimensions table in *appendix a*, see page 254.

solar storage vessels – questions and comments

Here are a few common questions and comments. As with the questions and comments in the solar collectors section of this book, the theories and opinions expressed are for guidance and should not be considered the definitive answer.

'a mains pressure solar hot water cylinder is better than a gravity-fed cylinder'
The main reasons given for this statement are:

it provides better water pressure for a shower

This could well be true but depends entirely on the mains water pressure being delivered to the property; a drop in this pressure has a direct impact on every hot water outlet fed from a mains pressure water-storage vessel, whereas a gravity-fed vessel benefits from a reservoir of constant pressure (albeit lower than mains pressure).

Also, there may be a significant drop in water pressure when more than one outlet is demanding water, converting a forceful shower into an unappealing dribble.

Gravity-fed hot water pressure to a shower can be boosted by a pump which, although it may consume a small amount of electricity, does have the advantage of ensuring all other hot water outlets are supplied with lower pressure water. This can result in lower water consumption and less dirty water passing into the sewage system; consider the wider environmental impact of gravity fed vs. mains pressure.

no cold water storage cistern so no frost risk

Those people unfortunate enough to have suffered a burst water pipe in a roof space will understand this reason. However, in the grand scheme of things, frost damage to water pipes and cold water storage cisterns in roof spaces is uncommon and usually the result of poorly-fitted insulation (or none at all).

There are guidelines on the installation of insulation to water pipes and vessels in unheated spaces to prevent frost damage, making this a particularly poor reason for determining which type of hot water storage vessel is best for you.

a quicker filling bath

In most cases, mains pressure hot water storage vessels will indeed fill a bath much quicker than a gravity-fed vessel. If you are a 'bath' person, this is as good a reason as any to choose mains pressure.

'a 200 litre solar thermal store will deliver all the hot water and space heating needed'

This is a bit misleading. The thermal store may well be capable of meeting the energy demanded, but it perhaps suggests that the solar is making the predominant contribution to space heating and hot water requirements, which is very unlikely.

Most of the energy required would instead be provided by another heat source (electric, gas, oil, etc) and in such a small thermal store (especially one delivering energy to a space heating system), it's quite likely that the solar contribution may actually be lower than an equivalent solar thermal system connected to a vented or unvented solar storage vessel supplying hot water only.

The higher than usual operating temperature in a thermal store, it's ability to draw heat from a fossil fuel heat source during daylight hours, and the turbulence caused within the store by fluid pumped around for space heating means that stratification has little opportunity to develop. This tends to have the effect of allowing the fossil fuel heat source to heat fluid in the lowest part of the store (the place where solar energy is to be delivered), perhaps raising the temperature to 50°C or more.

As a solar thermal system often operates on the basis of measuring temperature difference between collector and store, a store with a lowest temperature of 50°C will require a collector to generate more than 55°C before any solar contribution can be made.

In addition, a typical domestic property requires more energy to heat room space than to provide hot water, and at a time of year when there is much less solar radiation.

Solar simulation computer programmes estimate that the solar energy required to deliver even 15% of the annual combined hot water and space-heating energy for a typical modern, well-insulated home would require a thermal store well in excess of 200 litres. In European countries utilising solar contributions for space heating (typically those with generous grant funding), it is not uncommon for a domestic thermal store to hold 600-2000 litres.

circulation systems for solar thermal

There are essentially two methods for transporting heat from solar collectors to a storage vessel; both methods use a fluid as the heat transfer medium.

thermosiphon gravity circulation

Gravity circulation uses the natural buoyancy of hot fluid to move heat, see page 85, and requires:
- the solar collector to be below the storage vessel
- the heat transfer medium to move freely within the transmission pipes; a minimum pipe diameter ensuring low frictional resistance and there should be no valves or other devices with a small internal diameter such that they would restrict flow
- a steady supply of solar radiation to establish and maintain gravity circulation. In the UK, the regular passing of clouds can interrupt gravity circulation, reducing the transfer of heat

Gravity circulation requires no temperature sensing devices, pumps or controllers that would consume electricity, making the system very simple.

forced circulation

Accounting for the vast majority of solar thermal systems in the UK, forced circulation requires a circulating pump, a means of controlling when the pump is activated and a power source.

The benefits of forced circulation are:
- solar collectors do not have to be positioned below the storage vessel
- heat energy in the solar collector can be quickly moved to the storage vessel; this is particularly beneficial in locations experiencing changeable weather
- transmission pipes can be small in diameter, making pipes less obtrusive

differential temperature control

The most common method of controlling forced circulation in solar thermal systems, a **differential temperature controller** (DTC) compares the readings of temperature sensors mounted in the solar collector and storage vessel to activate a circulating pump.

This method is normally powered by alternating current (AC) electricity but direct current (DC) 12 volt battery-powered versions are also available.

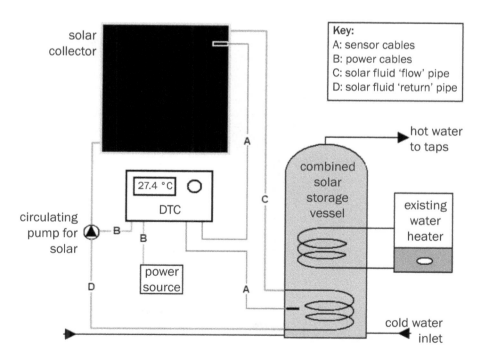

fig 46: differential temperature control

When the temperature in the solar collector rises above the temperature in the storage vessel (often programmable but typically +5 to +10 °C higher), the DTC provides power to the pump. This is called the 'switch on temperature differential' or 'T-ON'. Power to the pump will be stopped when this temperature difference falls (to around +2 to +4 °C). This is called the 'switch off temperature differential' or 'T-OFF'.

By controlling circulation based on temperature measurements, a DTC will:
- only consume the amount of power necessary to transfer heat energy as it becomes available
- avoid wasteful power consumption by the pump; for example at night
- reduce the negative effect of 'heat export'; this describes the active removal of heat from a storage vessel. Failure to manage 'heat export' can significantly reduce the solar benefit as previously-generated solar or fossil fuel heat within the storage vessel is circulated to and dissipated by a cooler solar collector (acting like a radiator).

There is also a 'maximum temperature for the storage vessel'. This safety function ensures that the storage vessel cannot be heated to dangerously high temperatures by the solar thermal system, and is often set to 60-65 °C. This is also called the 'T-MAX' temperature.

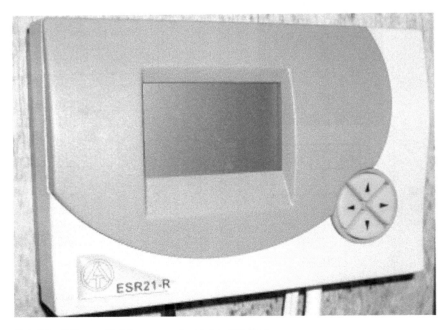

fig 47: differential temperature controller

fig 48: Thermomax differential temperature controller

light intensity control

A light-capturing device such as a light intensity sensor is used to activate the solar thermal system's circulating pump.

A light sensor captures light energy at a given location and passes this information to a controller, which in turn provides power to a circulating pump.

It is vital that a light-capturing device controlling a solar thermal system is installed in the same location and subject to the same light conditions as the solar thermal collector. Any difference in light intensity received by the light-capturing device and the solar collector (for example caused by shading or a different installation angle or orientation) could cause inappropriate supply of power to a circulating pump and thus reduce system performance.

There are light intensity control devices available powered by both AC and DC. Some designs replace the light sensor with a small photovoltaic panel, which is capable of providing variable DC power to a controller or, where a controller is omitted from the design, directly to a circulating pump.

Where a controller is included in the design, its purpose is to:
- provide power to a circulating pump once a preset light intensity has been recorded
- stop circulation (and therefore solar heat contributions to the storage vessel) once a preset maximum temperature has been recorded. This is done by a temperature sensor measuring the storage vessel temperature.

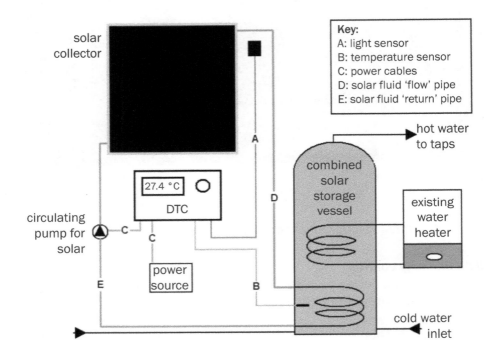

Key:
A: light sensor
B: temperature sensor
C: power cables
D: solar fluid 'flow' pipe
E: solar fluid 'return' pipe

fig 49: solar thermal system with light intensity controller

Fig 49 shows a light intensity controlled solar thermal system using a light sensor, controller and maximum temperature sensor for the storage vessel.

Fig 50 shows an example of a simple light intensity design using a photovoltaic panel to directly supply power to a circulating pump.

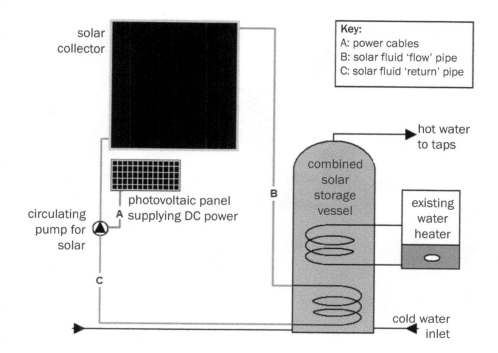

fig 50: *solar thermal system with photovoltaic panel*

circulating pumps

Forced circulation solar thermal systems can be powered by AC or DC electricity.

Circulating pumps are available to operate using AC or DC electricity though there is a wider range of AC-powered pumps suitable for use with solar thermal systems.

A good circulating pump for the task would:
- be made of materials that are tolerant to the highest likely operating temperatures or positioned in such a way that it is protected from temperature extremes
- consume a small amount of energy during circulation; typically less than 40 watts. This is because circulation needs to be relatively slow in a solar thermal system.
- be of durable construction. As the main moving part, the circulating pump is arguably the most likely component to fail.

fig 51: a typical AC-powered circulating pump for use with solar thermal systems, side view

fig 52: a typical AC-powered circulating pump for use with solar thermal systems, viewed from above

Some AC-powered circulating pumps are now available as part of a package of components, designed primarily to reduce installation time for solar thermal system installers.

These packages are known as 'pump stations' or 'pump groups' and feature several other key components. However, not all system designs require all of these components in order to work effectively (see *system design* chapter, page 125, for further details)

fig 53: completed pump station

Key:
A: circulating pump
B: flow-regulator
C: pressure gauge
D: pressure relief valve
E: filling connections
F: combined valves
     non-return valves
     isolating valve
     bypass thermometer
G: expansion vessel
connection
H: degassing chamber

fig 54: pump station with insulated cover removed showing various components including circulating pump

flow control

The rate at which fluid passes through a solar collector has a bearing on the amount of heat energy added during a single pass and also the operating efficiency of the collector - too slow and the collector will gradually become hotter, and hotter collectors can lose more heat; too fast and the fluid doesn't absorb enough heat energy on each pass.

Flow control attempts to optimise the fluid flow rate and therefore the system operating efficiency. There are essentially two methods:

fixed flow rate

The flow is set according to the optimum rate specified by the solar collector manufacturer. As solar radiation is variable throughout the day an averaged flow rate is used to maximise system efficiency.

This method uses a fixed speed circulating pump, a simple differential temperature controller (DTC) and a flow regulator, which is adjusted to restrict the flow down to the required optimum rate, normally measured in litres per minute. Fig 55 shows a typical flow regulator with sight glass measuring flow in litres per minute. The slotted screw head is used to set the flow rate.

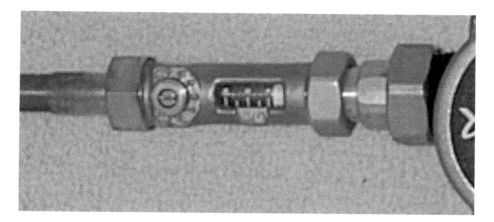

fig 55: a typical flow regulator

fixed flow rate system in operation

As the sun rises, the solar collector starts to heat up. When the simple DTC measures a temperature difference between the collector and storage vessel equal to 'T-ON', the circulating pump is given electricity.

The flow rate caused by the circulating pump at this point is too high to optimise system efficiency (fluid is passing through the collector too quickly). Therefore, the flow is reduced to a preset rate as it passes through the flow regulator (this adjustment is only required once, when the equipment is first installed).

When the collector cools sufficiently, the simple DTC will stop electricity to the circulating pump once a temperature difference equal to 'T-OFF' has been reached.

The simple DTC will activate and deactivate circulation as the amount of solar radiation (and therefore the amount of heat energy generated in the solar collector) varies over the course of each day.

variable flow rate

The flow rate is constantly varied to match the amount of solar energy captured by the solar collector. Rather than setting flow rate with a flow regulator, the function is performed by a DTC or photovoltaic panel rationing the amount of electricity passed to the circulating pump.

light-intensity-controlled systems

Where forced circulation is controlled directly by irradiance falling on a photovoltaic panel and where no temperature sensing is installed, the sizing of the photovoltaic panel is critical to ensure the correct flow rate of heat transfer medium.

Where forced circulation is controlled indirectly by a light sensor, circulation will start once a preset irradiance level has been measured.

differential temperature controlled (DTC) systems

Electricity is passed to the circulating pump proportional to the temperature difference between the solar collector and the storage vessel.

When the solar collector's temperature sensor records a difference equal to 'T-ON' the DTC will activate the circulating pump.

The more complex DTC used for this system is capable of passing AC electricity proportional to the measured temperature difference between the collector and storage vessel. Therefore, if this difference is small (for example the collector is just 10°C warmer), the electricity passed to the circulating pump will also be small.

This is achieved by 'pulsing' electricity to the circulating pump; at low temperature differences this could be pulsing equivalent to 30% electricity, rising in 10% increments to 100% as the temperature difference increases.

Using this method, the circulating pump will switch on and off less often during daylight hours and could potentially use less AC electricity to transfer the same amount of heat energy from collector to storage vessel.

Although flow is adjusted automatically by the rationing of electricity, removing the need for a flow regulator, one may still be fitted purely as a visual aid during essential installation maintenance checks.

non-return valves

These mechanical valves are designed to prevent unwanted movement of fluid by only allowing fluid under forced circulation to pass through in a single direction. An internal spring or hinged flap reseats the valve's sealing plate when forced circulation stops.

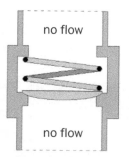
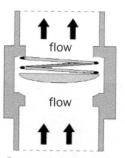

no flow

flow

flow

no flow

Pump deactivated: spring forces sealing disc in valve to close and stop flow in any direction

Pump activated: forced fluid pushes against sealing disc and spring to allow fluid to flow past

fig 56: non-return valve

Certain system designs will require one or more non-return valves (also known as check valves) to be installed to prevent uncontrolled circulation.

This is particularly important where the fluid pipes are installed in such a way that could allow heat to rise from the storage vessel to a solar collector when circulation is not wanted.

A good example of this would be at night when, without a non-return valve, heated fluid may be able to establish gravity circulation within the solar heat transfer pipes, causing heat in the storage vessel to be 'radiated' back to the night sky by the solar collector, therefore wasting previously captured renewable energy.

expansion system

As sunlight heats a solar collector, the heat transfer medium within the collector begins to expand. This expansion is the result of the warmed fluid becoming less dense and expanding, which inevitably displaces fluid surrounding it.

All system designs must, for reasons of safety and performance, allow this displaced fluid to move to another location to avoid the risk of rupturing pipes through over-pressure.

This is achieved in various ways and the devices used to manage fluid expansion may include:

expansion vessel

This steel vessel contains a flexible rubber membrane that separates a gas chamber from a heat-transfer-medium chamber.

fig 57: expansion vessel

In a sealed and pressurised circuit of fluid-filled pipes, an expansion vessel is used to hold the volume of fluid displaced by heat expansion. As this happens, the volume in the fluid chamber increases and pushes against the rubber membrane, compressing the gas on the other side. When the fluid cools down and contracts, the compressed gas (usually air or nitrogen) pushes against the rubber membrane and forces fluid back into the pipe circuit.

Expansion vessels are available in different sizes and for different purposes. The appropriate size of an expansion vessel is relative to the size, quantity and type of solar collectors and so is best specified as part of a package of components. There is an expansion vessel sizing guide in *appendix b*, see page 255.

drainback vessel

Designed for use in a drainback solar thermal system (see *whole systems section*, page 144) where fluid is allowed to drain out of the solar collector under certain operating conditions, a drainback vessel is essentially a chamber with a number of connecting pipes. In its simplest form, it can be a metal container where fluid enters from the top and leaves from the bottom.

fig 58: a sample drainback vessel with a section of metal wall and insulation cut away

Expansion of heated fluid is managed by the constant presence of an air pocket, which gathers inside the drainback vessel when circulation of fluid occurs and exits when circulation stops (the air is displaced upwards into the pipes and collector above the drainback vessel by fluid that is draining down from the solar collector).

feed and expansion tank

This fluid-holding tank is installed at the top of a solar thermal system and is open to atmospheric pressure, see the example shown in fig 91, page 145.

Operation is similar to that of an expansion vessel except that the fluid is not under pressure. Therefore, displaced fluid that enters the tank will return to the transfer pipes by the force of gravity rather than because a pressurised gas chamber is acting on it.

The feed and expansion tank was a common part of solar thermal systems in the UK up to around the 1980s but is now less popular. This is partly because the tank is open to the atmosphere and some heat transfer medium can readily evaporate, so that system-fluid level inspections and top-ups are required more frequently.

pressure relief valve

In the event of a fault occurring in a sealed circuit of pipes, a device should be available to discharge excess fluid pressure and avoid damage.

This is the task of a pressure relief valve; it is the designed 'weak point' in a system and so should discharge fluid at a preset pressure - lower than the maximum operating pressure of any other fluid-filled component.

fig 59: pressure relief valves

Pressure relief valves used in solar thermal systems can be placed in a selection of locations within the fluid circuit provided they are capable of withstanding the highest system temperature (for example a pressure relief valve mounted adjacent to a solar collector will get hotter than one installed next to the circulating pump) and no functional part of the valve degrades beyond effective use if subjected to the sunlight (plastic parts installed externally and without protection will often deteriorate under ultraviolet light).

Common valve pressure ratings (the pressure at which the valve starts to open and discharge) for solar thermal systems are 3 bar and 6 bar.

pressure gauge

This gauge provides a means of observing fluid pressure within a sealed circuit of pipes. The scale can be expressed in a variety of terms but most commonly the *bar* scale is stated. There is a conversion table for different expressions of pressure in *appendix d*, see page 257.

fig 60: pressure gauge – front and back views

A pressure gauge is only required for system designs that allow heat transfer medium to be pressurised beyond normal atmospheric pressure under all working conditions.

insulation

Once a solar collector has captured useful heat energy, it must be transferred to the storage vessel and held until hot water is needed.
The circuit of pipes and other components used to carry the heat transfer

medium will all absorb some heat energy as the fluid is circulated, and this is unavoidable. However, once heated, these components will also start to emit some of this energy to the surrounding air and so there is a need to provide some form of insulation.

Most components in a solar thermal system should have insulation applied to limit the amount of heat loss, with a few exceptions:

Components that must be protected from high temperature because they contain rubber or plastic parts should not be insulated and they include:
- expansion vessel, and the pipe leading to it; by not adding insulation, heat is intentionally allowed to dissipate through the walls of the pipe leading to the vessel (see expansion vessel section, page 101)
- drain cocks; these provide convenient fluid draining points in the circuit of pipes. Drain cocks are a standard plumbing component and are not designed for solar temperatures; if used, protect from heat by installing at the end of a downward pointing uninsulated branch of pipe (also known as a dead leg).
- circulating pump and other electrical components; some are designed to be partially insulated and if so, will be supplied with the insulation. Most circulating pumps and electrical components will overheat and may present a fire risk if insulated.

types of insulation

There are four main types of insulation material available in the UK that are (or have been) used on solar thermal systems:

polyethylene pipe insulation

This is the least expensive and most widely available material, found in most hardware and DIY stores.

Typically grey, white or green in colour, it is a standard plumbing product that is only suitable for low-temperature solar thermal systems. When installed on high temperature systems, this insulation has been found to melt off pipes, leaving them uninsulated.

The material will also break down in the presence of ultraviolet light, making it unsuitable for use outdoors unless it is covered. Polyethylene insulation is unaffected if it gets wet and retains the same insulating properties as when it is dry.

fig 61: *polyethylene insulation*

elastomeric insulation

Mainly available in pre-formed pipe insulation but can sometimes be obtained in sheet form, the elastomeric insulation range includes:
high temperature elastomeric insulation which is tolerant to the temperatures experienced in solar thermal systems, is very flexible, stable under ultraviolet light and suffers no detrimental effects when wet. It can be difficult to obtain; rarely available in hardware or DIY stores
fig 62: high temperature elastomeric insulation

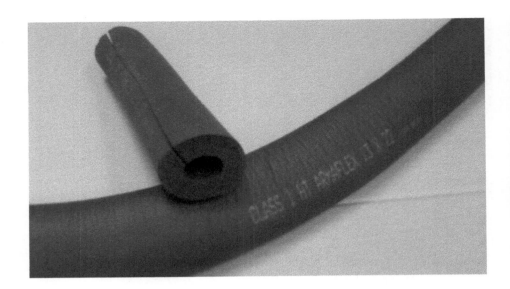

medium temperature elastomeric insulation is less tolerant to high temperatures (but can be used in certain 'cooler' areas of solar thermal systems), is very flexible, suffers no bad effects when wet but is not stable in ultraviolet light, so shouldn't be used outdoors (it eventually turns to a coarse dust).

fig 63: medium temperature elastomeric insulation

This type of insulation is often available from good plumbing stores or refrigeration equipment suppliers and rarely available from hardware or DIY stores.

foil-faced mineral wool insulation

Widely available in plumbing merchants but rare in hardware or DIY stores, foil-faced mineral wool insulation is commonly used in industrial plumbing and heating installations.

fig 64: foil-faced mineral wool insulation

The material is highly temperature tolerant (to temperatures that are far higher than is experienced in solar thermal systems), easy to cut and manipulate, is stable in ultraviolet light and has good insulating properties. However, if allowed to get wet the material begins to lose its insulation value and is therefore not the best choice for use outdoors.

pipework

transmission pipes

As modern solar collectors are capable of generating temperatures well in excess of 100°C, heat transfer medium must be moved from collector to storage vessel using transmission pipes able to withstand these conditions. Transmission pipes consist of pipes, fittings and fixing clips.

plastic pipes, fittings and clips

These are generally unsuitable for use in solar thermal systems for hot water due mainly to the likelihood of the heat transfer medium exceeding the maximum design temperature of the material, which is rarely more than

110°C (depending on the type of plastic).

Industry experience has shown that plastic components used in solar transmission pipe systems are unreliable, often causing fluid loss under conditions of high solar irradiance and low hot water demand.

Exceptions include the use of plastic pipes in low temperature solar applications (such as swimming pool solar thermal systems) or where plastic clips are used to retain transmission pipes but do not make contact with high temperature surfaces (such as clips secured around pipe insulation enclosing a high temperature pipe).

fig 65: plastic pipe and fittings

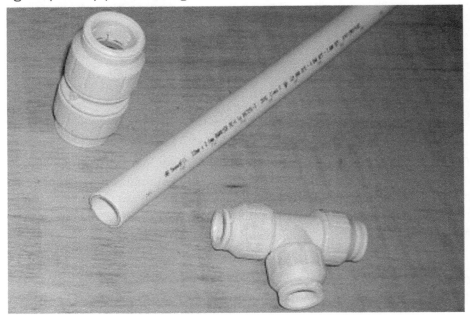

rubber pipes

A limited number of transmission pipes used in solar hot water systems are made from a rubber compound.

The exact composition of the rubber will determine the material's ability to withstand high temperatures and there may be explicit manufacturer's instructions for its use.

As these products tend to be unique to a particular design of solar thermal system, it's generally unwise to adapt such materials for use in other designs without an adequate understanding of the consequences.

Fittings and clips for joining together and securing rubber transmission pipes are normally made from metal.

metal pipes, fittings and clips

Metal is the most common material used in transmission pipes, fittings and clips. Copper tubing with copper or brass solder fittings are particularly popular, and are suitable for many solar hot water system designs subject to:

- the solder used does not contain a potentially harmful substance (such as lead) if used on drinking quality water
- the solder used is reliable at foreseeable collector temperatures; lead solder has a melting point of around 185°C and lead-free solder around 230°C.

fig 66: copper tubing with copper end-feed solder fittings

Copper tubing may also be connected using brass compression fittings. In this case, the fittings will provide adequate temperature tolerance but will need to be reliable under all foreseeable operating pressures. This may involve the use of special metal-pipe-reinforcing inserts at pressures above 3 bar.

fig 67: copper tubing with brass compression fittings

In recent years, press-fit fittings have been developed for use with copper tubing. Press-fit fittings have been used in commercial applications for some time on conventional plumbing arrangements but were not previously capable of withstanding the combined pressures and temperatures associated with solar energy systems.

Fittings are now available with special rubber O-ring inserts suitable for high temperature solar pipes.

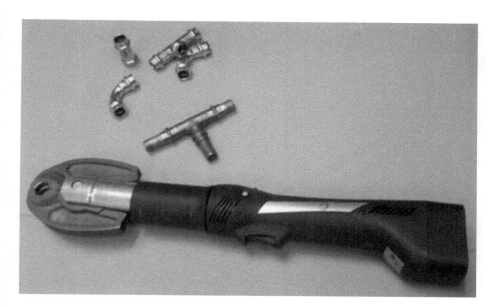

fig 68: press-fit fittings

Due to the limited availability of the fittings and the high cost of the tools, press-fit fittings are currently only used by some specialist solar energy installers.

Stainless steel flexible pipes are sometimes employed where transmission pipe routes are awkward or installation speed is critical. As the full length of these pipes is flexible, obstacles can be easily negotiated and fittings are only needed at each end.

fig 69: press-fit tool

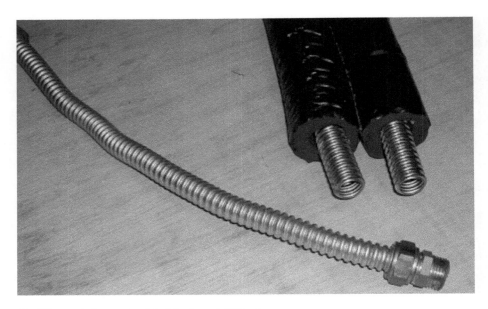

fig 70: stainless steel tubing and fittings

Stainless steel tubing is only available from specialist suppliers though some larger plumbing suppliers can now order these items.

Whilst the cost of stainless steel tubing is higher than copper, it is available in a range of time-saving formats including pre-insulated and fitted with a high temperature cable for connection of the collector's temperature sensor.

The crossover from stainless steel flexible tubing to conventional fittings and pipes is via an adaptive fitting which employs a special high-temperature tolerant fibre washer or gasket. To ensure a durable connection it is essential that only solar-rated fibre washers or gaskets are used; many other fibre washers or gaskets are available but they are not suitable.

One disadvantage of stainless steel tubing lies in its design. The corrugation which allows for bending of the tube without breaking creates resistance to the movement of fluid inside the pipe. This resistance may require the use of a larger diameter tube compared to copper.

In addition, the corrugation has a tendency to trap small air bubbles which can increase the time taken to purge air and commission the system; particularly in the case of fully-filled solar primary circuits, see *whole system* section, page 144.

filling and commissioning components

The following components and methods can help when filling a solar thermal system with fluid and preparing for normal operation.

air separator (also occasionally known as a de-gasser)
Essentially a large chamber that encourages air to separate from fluid that is passing through the chamber, an air separator is installed as part of the solar thermal system's fluid-carrying pipe circuit and is useful on systems that are to be fully filled with fluid (this does not apply to drainback systems). The top of the air separator has either manual or automatic air release devices.

Some designs of air separator feature an internal micro-bubble separation device such as a wire mesh or fine wires arranged like the bristles on a cylindrical hair brush. Other designs adopt a simpler method of separation using one or more deflectors to agitate the flow of liquid in the chamber.

fig 71: brass air separator (shown here with isolating valve and stainless steel automatic air vent on top)

automatic air vent

This vent is a small chamber containing a float-operated valve which allows air to be automatically released but prevents heat transfer medium from escaping.

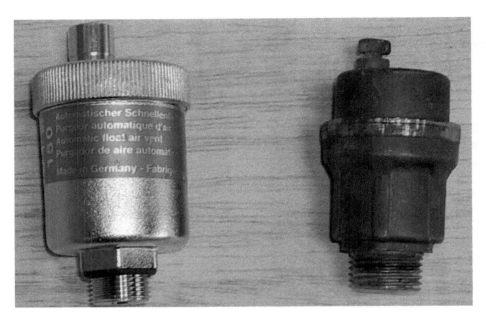

fig 72: stainless steel and brass automatic air vents

An automatic air vent can be attached to the top of an air separator or installed alone at high points in a circuit of pipes. It is only useful on systems that are fully filled with fluid; some systems do not need to have air purged from them, see *whole systems* section, page 144.

Automatic air vents are widely available from plumbing stores but it should be noted that these models are likely to use a plastic internal float. High-temperature tolerant, stainless steel vents are available from solar thermal equipment suppliers.

air release cap

This simple device comprises a screw cap that allows small amounts of air to be manually released from fluid-filled pipes. They are available in a variety of designs, some of which contain hidden plastic or rubber seals and so are not tolerant of high temperatures.

fig 73: air release cap (circled)

filling bottle

A means of filling a circuit of pipes with heat transfer medium under pressure (which could be water or a water/antifreeze mix), a filling bottle is a simple way of adding fluid without the need for expensive specialist equipment and is often adapted from a garden sprayer. This component does not form part of the permanent installation.

fig 74: A good garden sprayer is often designed to pressurise fluid up to 3 bar so makes a handy tool for the job of filling a pressurised solar thermal system

pipework pressure-testing pump

This is a conventional plumbing tool which can be used to fill and pressurise a solar water heating system. Though not capable of easily purging the system of air, this type of pump can be readily rented from a tool hire shop.

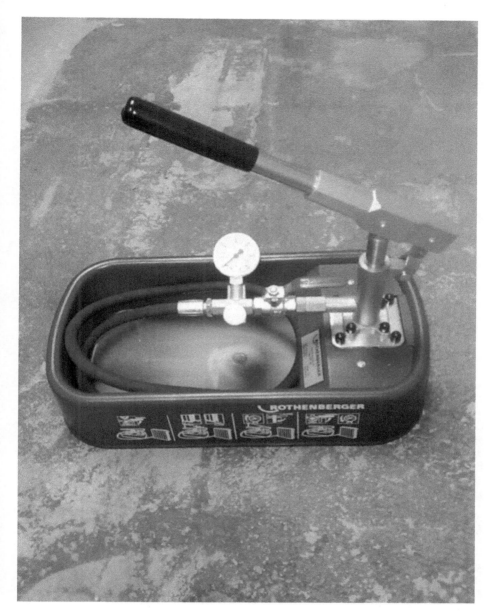

fig 75: pipework pressure testing pump

solar thermal system filling and commissioning machine
A specialist machine which allows the user to rapidly fill a pressurised circuit
with heat transfer medium, whilst at the same time purging the fluid-filled
circuit of air.

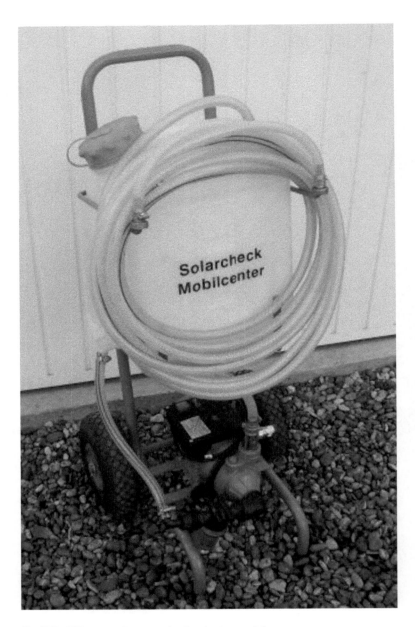

fig 76: filling and commissioning machine

These machines are only used by professional solar thermal installers due mainly to the machine's cost and availability; they are not normally available from tool hire shops. This component does not form part of the permanent installation.

cold water filling loop

This describes a branch pipe leading from the main cold water supply in a house. A series of valves are placed along the pipe to prevent accidental contamination of the cold water source by heat transfer medium flowing in the wrong direction, and a flexible pipe is used to temporarily connect the filling loop to an inlet valve on the solar thermal system's fluid pipes and is suitable for filling pressurised and non-pressurised solar thermal systems with water. If the heat transfer medium also requires antifreeze, this must be added as a concentrate at an alternative point.

fig 77: cold water filling loop (circled)

I wouldn't recommend the use of cold water filling loops on systems requiring antifreeze. This is because if a fault occurs and some fluid is discharged, there is a temptation to simply open the filling loop and 'top up' the heat transfer medium with pure water. This has the result of diluting antifreeze and therefore reducing the solar collector's frost protection (an expensive component to replace!).

heat transfer medium

Some solar thermal systems use an antifreeze solution to protect external components from the effects of frost. Other designs rely solely on pure cold water, see *whole systems* section, page 144.

antifreeze solutions

In this case, the antifreeze used is normally propylene glycol. This type of glycol has the benefit of being low in toxicity (unlike ethylene glycol which is much more toxic), will readily blend with water and is often tolerant to high temperatures (the manufacturer will advise the precise maximum temperature).

fig 78: a range of propylene glycol solutions available for solar thermal systems

Glycol suitable for solar thermal systems will often be available in two forms; a premixed solution or a concentrate. The concentrate has the benefit of offering different levels of frost protection according to the mix ratio with cold water whilst the premixed solution can be easier to use.

Properties of propylene glycol at a glance:

- stable under sustained temperatures exceeding 160°C (product dependent)
- frost protection down to -30°C (subject to mix ratio)
- contains corrosion inhibitors
- particularly suitable for use in solar systems where the fluid is sealed (rather than open vented)
- compatible with most rubber composites found in plumbing components including: SBR,NBR, EPDM, PTFE (product dependent)
- can appear translucent or coloured (depending on product)
- lower heat-carrying capacity than pure water
- dissolves zinc in galvanised metal coatings

pure water as a heat transfer medium

If you live in an area that is subject to sub-zero temperatures, frost is clearly an issue for solar collectors. Systems using pure water as a heat transfer medium employ means other than antifreeze to protect the solar collector and external pipes from possible frost damage.

These may include:

- a differential temperature controller with a special function that circulates heat from the storage vessel to keep the solar collector 'artificially' warm
- a system design that allows all pure water to drain out of the collector and adjoining pipes into a reservoir installed in a heated part of the building, see *whole systems: drainback, page 144* for further details
- a solar collector and adjoining pipes made of a material that does not suffer damage when water freezes

system design

Solar water heating is essentially a 'demand driven' technology and the ratio of solar collector size to storage vessel size is important to ensure a comfortable hot water temperature, a useful volume of hot water and to help improve the durability of other system components and materials.

calculating hot water demand

How much hot water does your home use in a day? This isn't normally a simple question to answer accurately and so a good estimate is often the best we can achieve.

An estimate can be made by assuming that most household occupants will consume between 15 and 55 litres of hot water (at 60°C) per day, and a figure that falls somewhere in this range can be chosen for each occupant depending on their attitude to water and energy conservation.

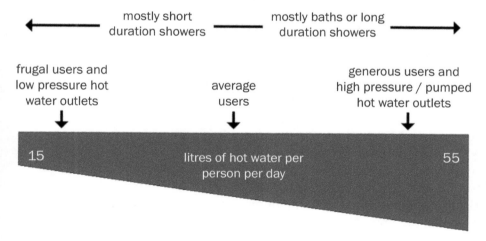

fig 79: range of water usage

Each home will use hot water in different ways; here are some points to consider when estimating consumption:
• some people prefer to bath rather than shower
• how many regular occupants there are
• consider the number of times a week a washing machine is used and whether it is filled using stored hot water

- remember to include hot water used in hand basins and kitchen sinks
- consider how often a dishwasher is used and whether it is filled using stored hot water
- remember that stored hot water is normally diluted with some cold water when used. This means that 20 litres of hot water at 60°C becomes more than 30 litres of hot water at shower temperature.

a note on water consumption:

Hot water on tap in UK homes has been commonplace for many decades now and often little regard is paid to the energy needed to process water to an acceptably clean standard, deliver the water under pressure to homes and then heat the water for use in baths, sinks and showers.

In recent years there has been a trend towards higher flow rates to showers but before deciding on a high flow, high volume solar hot water storage vessel to supply a powerful shower, it may be useful to quantify just a small part of the impact of the decision.

A table illustrating this is shown in the *appendix*, see page 256, and remember – the table doesn't include the additional cost of energy to heat water (which will vary depending on fuel type used).

Here are some approximate volumes of 60°C hot water consumed in the home:
- kitchen bowl (for washing dishes) = 4.5 litres
- standard-sized bath = 50 litres
- low flow shower = 2.5 litres per minute
- medium flow shower = 3.5 litres per minute
- high flow shower = 5 litres per minute
- very high flow shower = 7 litres per minute

Using the figures above and the number of hot water users normally in the property, two important figures can be estimated:
- the peak hot water demand
- the total daily hot water demand

peak demand (Vp)

Peak demand relates to the time of day when most hot water is likely to be used simultaneously before the backup water heater has an opportunity to switch on and heat more stored water to the required temperature.

Peak demand will determine the minimum volume of water that can be heated by a backup water heater. This is essential for comfort and convenience as the backup water heater is the main source of hot water during periods of poor solar radiation such as cloudy winter days.

This minimum volume can be larger than the peak demand estimated, but it's worth noting that increasing the volume capable of being heated by a fossil-fuel-powered water heater in a single heating cycle could mean:
- the backup water heater will take longer to heat the larger volume to a useful temperature (known as the recovery or reheat time)
- there will be excess hot water regularly held in the storage vessel; more fossil-fuel sourced heat stored for longer periods means greater heat loss that damages the environment and costs you money
- if you are limited for space in which to fit the storage vessel, it could result in less water volume for the solar thermal system to heat; this reduces the clean and free annual energy contribution from the solar equipment

The following diagram, fig 80, shows the path of cold water through to the household hot water outlets.

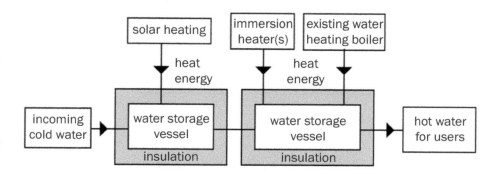

fig 80: path of water through the system

The volume of stored water receiving solar heat energy and the volume of stored water receiving backup heat energy (from a boiler or immersion heater) can be separate or combined.

This portion of the stored hot water volume should be at least equal to the peak demand (Vp).

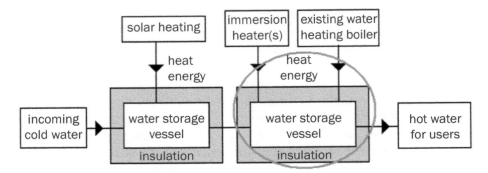

fig 81: total peak demand (Vp)

total daily demand (Vd)

This is the volume of hot water that is consumed in an *average* day by all of the building's usual occupants.

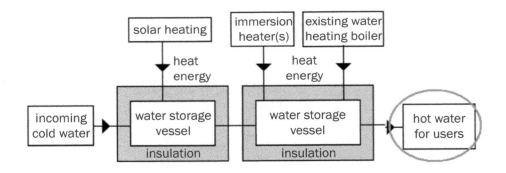

fig 82: total daily demand (Vd)

In addition to peak demand and total daily demand, there are two more important volumes to note.

total stored hot water volume(Vt)

This is the sum of water stored that can be heated by any type of fuel source (solar + backup heaters), fig 83 illustrates this.

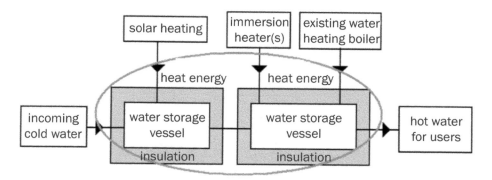

fig 83: total stored hot water volume (Vt)

dedicated solar volume(Vs)

This is the volume of stored water that can only be heated by solar energy, it is circled in fig 84.

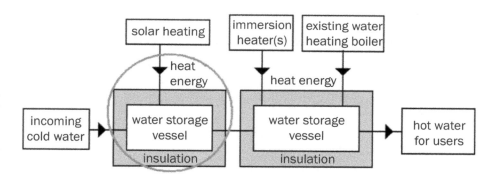

fig 84: volume of water heated only by solar energy (Vs)

dedicated solar volume in a separate storage vessel

The volume of the storage vessel on the right of fig 85 is determined by peak demand. The storage vessel on the left is dedicated to solar-only energy input and would ideally hold a volume of up to the equivalent of the daily hot water demand. A volume less than equivalent to the daily hot water demand can be considered but a low volume will reduce overall energy provided by the solar equipment. A volume larger than the daily volume can also be considered but may reduce the number of occasions solar reaches its target water temperature (TMAX: see *differential temperature control* section, page 91) and should be balanced against the desire to limit the risk of bacterial growth (daily consumption of the entire solar heated water volume can help limit this).

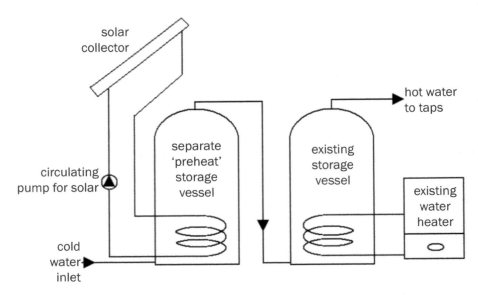

fig 85: water heated by solar energy stored in a separate vessel

dedicated solar volume in a combined storage vessel

Fig 86 shows a twin-coil storage vessel. The existing water heater can heat all water above the lowest part of its heat exchanger (shown here as an internal coil). This volume should be equal to or greater than the peak demand volume.

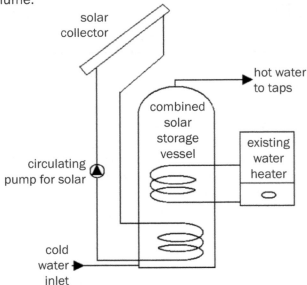

fig 86: dedicated solar volume in a combined storage vessel

The solar thermal system can potentially heat all water above the lowest part of its heat exchanger which, being located at the very bottom of the storage vessel, is the entire contents of the vessel. However, only the volume below the lowest part of the backup water heater's heat exchanger is regarded as the dedicated solar volume. This dedicated solar volume should be equal to or less than the total daily hot water demand.

Where a combined storage vessel is used it is particularly important to remember that the smaller the dedicated solar volume, the smaller the potential contribution from solar will be, particularly when the backup water heater is allowed to make a heat contribution during sunshine hours.

There are exceptions to these general sizing rules as some solar hot water systems use the existing hot water cylinder, which often has only a single heat exchange coil connected to the backup water heater.

In this case, water is either circulated directly (no heat exchanger or separate fluid) through the solar collector and back to the cylinder, or a heat exchanger is fitted to the top or side of the cylinder.

As there is no volume of stored water that is dedicated to solar energy (the backup water heater can potentially heat the same volume of water as solar), there is a critical requirement to ensure that the backup heater is well controlled and not allowed to contribute heat before each evening (after the solar has had an opportunity to deliver energy during daylight hours).

Failure to address this issue can result in the backup water heater displacing most of the potential solar energy benefit. This is because the backup water heater has a larger instantaneous energy output and so can deliver heat energy faster than solar, leaving nowhere for water heated by solar energy to be accumulated.

examples of storage vessel sizing

Here are two scenarios to help explain the sum of volumes that determine the final storage vessel size. For simplicity, peak demand volumes shown here assume the backup water heater is not able to reheat water during the peak demand time period. In practice, the backup water heater might well be replenishing some of the stored heat simultaneously as hot water is used. This would have the effect of reducing the peak demand volume required in the storage vessel.

important note on peak demand volume

Where a bath is installed in a building but seldom used, it might be a good idea to base peak demand on the volume of the bath plus the volume consumed by any other outlet likely to draw off hot water simultaneously (such as a kitchen sink). In the following text, this is referred to as 'volume X'; although it is not strictly the peak demand volume on a *typical* day it is a practical alternative to ensure users can conveniently run a full bath of water.

scenario a

- 2 adult occupants
- average hot water users (35 litres per person per day at 60°C)
- about 70% of the hot water use is in the morning

2 x 35 = 70 litres total daily demand (Vd)
70 x 70% = 49 litres peak demand (Vp) *or* volume X (whichever is appropriate)

Dedicated solar volume (Vs) is recommended to be 80 to 100% of total daily demand:

70 x 80% = 56 litres
70 x 100% = 70 litres

So, the hot water volumes might look like this:

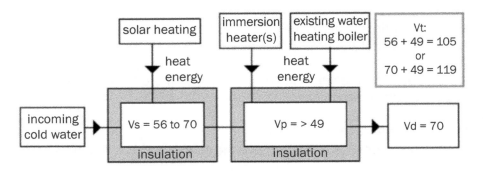

fig 87: possible hot water volumes for scenario a

Don't forget: Vp shown here is a *minimum* of 49 litres, see important note on Vp, above, and Vs is a recommended range (local regulations may set a mandatory level lower than this).

scenario b

- 2 adult and 3 child occupants
- slightly above average hot water users (45 litres per person per day)
- about 30% of the hot water use is in the morning, 10% during the day and 60% in the evening

5 x 45 = 225 litres total daily demand (Vd)
225 x 60% = 135 litres peak demand (Vp) **or** volume X (whichever is appropriate)

Dedicated solar volume (Vs) is recommended to be 80% to 100% of total daily demand:

225 x 80% = 180 litres
225 x 100% = 225 litres

So, the hot water volumes might look like this:

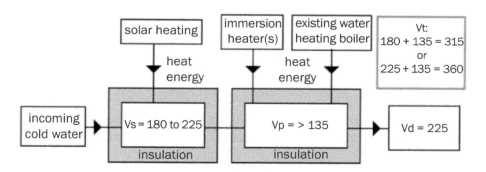

fig 88: possible hot water volumes for scenario b

Don't forget: Vp shown here is a *minimum* of 135 litres, see important note on volume X, page 132, and Vs is a recommended range (local regulations may set a mandatory level lower than this).

solar contribution

This is the amount of annual hot water demand that is met by solar energy.

Solar thermal systems in the UK are often designed to supply over 90% of domestic hot water demand in the peak summer months and this method generally means an annual solar contribution of 30 to 60%, with most of this energy (about three quarters of the annual contribution) coming between the start of April and the end of September. The backup water heater provides the remaining energy.

In general, the solar contribution can be improved by choosing a storage vessel with a total volume at the larger end of the range outlined above (subject to the physical dimensions of the storage vessel location, see *appendix a* for cylinder volumes/dimensions page 254), and improved further still where a greater percentage of the total volume can only be heated by solar (rather than a backup water heater).

solar collector sizing

There are many ways to work out the quantity and size of collector needed and they vary in complexity.

The ratio of 'solar collector surface area' to 'storage volume that can be heated by solar energy' is all-important.

Too large a collector surface area and the system may generate excessive hot water temperatures in summer, and more frequently subject components to the potentially harmful effects of very high temperature heat transfer medium, thus reducing overall system reliability.

Too small a collector surface area and the system will deliver less than optimal solar energy, forcing the backup heat source to contribute more frequently.

Before selecting a method, consider the variable nature of the solar resource, the assumptions used to estimate important influencing factors (such as hot water consumption) and how much time you want to spend working it out.

starting with basics

The size of a solar collector can be defined in four ways:
- the physical width, length, height and depth (not normally used if energy output is stated)
- the gross surface area; a footprint of the entire collector measured in square metres
- the absorber surface area; a footprint of the absorbing surface alone, ignoring any surrounding area occupied by insulation, air gaps or structural elements of the collector

- the aperture surface area; a footprint of the surface area that light can pass through to reach the absorber. This footprint includes any mirrors used to reflect light.

Aperture surface area is generally the best reference for calculating the required size and quantity of solar collectors at this stage of the design.

construction method

As described in the *solar collectors* chapter, see page 33, the method of construction and materials used will also have a direct impact on energy output.

A home-made solar collector will deliver a smaller energy output for any given size due to greater heat loss and lower light absorption from:
- gaps in insulation material
- gaps in the collector casing
- less efficient heat transfer from the absorber fins to the heat transfer medium
- the probable use of matt black paint on the absorber instead of selective surface coating
- the probable use of glazing materials that reduce the amount of light passing through to the absorber

A collector design requiring absorbed solar radiation to pass through a series of heat exchangers before reaching the tap water to be heated may also reduce overall energy output, or have the effect of 'delaying' energy contribution as the thermal mass of materials at each stage of the heat transfer process absorbs some of the energy being transported.

Certain heat-pipe evacuated-tube collectors provide an example of this; solar radiation striking the absorber surface must pass through one or more glass layers to an aluminium fin, then a copper tube to an initial heat transfer fluid, then back through the copper tube to another copper tube before passing into the final heat transfer medium which circulates to the storage vessel.

sizing methods

Where the following sizing methods state a surface area range, consider collector design and construction when deciding whether to use a larger or smaller surface area from the range specified.

If you are comparing factory-made solar collectors and have access to BS EN12975-2 test reports you can get an indication of relative performance from key data within the report, see the *solar collectors* chapter, page 33.

method 1: simple rule of thumb

At its simplest, average output for most locations in mainland Britain can be assumed to conform to the following rule of thumb:

- **flat plate collectors** 1.0 square metre for each hot water user
- **evacuated tube collectors** 0.7 square metre for each hot water user

This simple rule of thumb makes assumptions about the amount of hot water each user consumes, and ignores the difference in collector performance based on quality of construction.

From this starting point, the figure should be adjusted to allow for site conditions: shading, orientation etc. as follows.

method 2: sizing according to collector type and hot water use

This method attempts to size collectors using average performance characteristics of similar groups of products and relates to hot water demand rather than the number of users. It is a more detailed way of sizing a domestic solar hot water system without access to computer simulation software.

First, select the initial aperture surface area for the chosen type of collector. To do this, you will need to choose the description that best matches your collector from the following table.

collector type	collector initial surface area (m² per 30 litres of dedicated solar volume)
Glazed and insulated factory-made flat plate with selective surface absorber	0.9 to 1.2
Glazed and insulated factory-made collector with matt black painted absorber	1.0 to 1.3
Glazed and insulated home-made flat plate collector with matt black painted absorber	1.3 to 1.6
Direct flow evacuated tube collector	0.7 to 0.9
Heat pipe evacuated tube collector	0.7 to 1.1

Note: The ranges in the table above allow for differences in optical (light transmission) and thermal (heat transfer and emission) performance of individual products within a group. Where performance of the chosen collector is known to be lower than similar products within the group, an initial surface area at the upper end of the range should be chosen.

The results of using method 1 or 2 should now be adjusted as required according to the following local conditions.

light reaching the absorber surface of a collector

Lots of factors can limit the amount of solar radiation striking the surface of the absorber. These include:

UK location

Solar radiation as direct sunlight (direct beam radiation on a clear day) is more intense than diffuse sunlight (indirect sunlight scattered by particles and water droplets in the atmosphere). One location close to the sea may regularly experience more clouds and mist than another location further along the coast, which can reduce overall solar irradiance striking the collector.

Select the geographical location for the collector installation from the map in fig 89 and adjust the initial surface area accordingly. For information on locations outside of Great Britain, see *resources*, page 263.

Note: when selecting your location, be aware that certain geographical conditions can significantly reduce the amount of daylight striking a solar collector. An example would be a building whose sunlight is partially obscured by steep hills.

orientation of collector

A solar collector absorbs the most amount of energy when its entire absorber surface is directly exposed to solar radiation. As the sun follows a path across the sky from east to west, this would only be possible if a solar collector were installed on a frame that could be turned to 'track' the sun's apparent movement. In reality, this is highly impractical and therefore an optimum orientation is used to maximise energy output from a static solar collector. This optimum orientation is achieved by pointing the collector towards the equator.

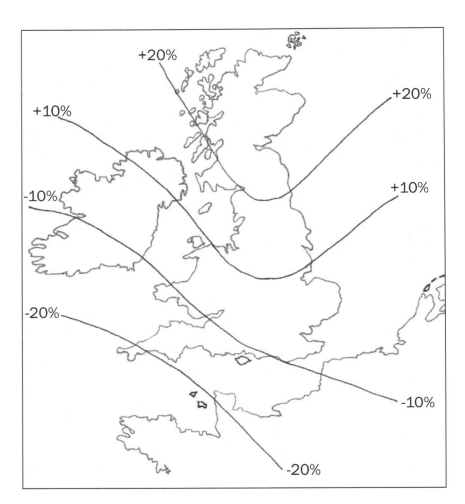

fig 89: effect of location on available solar radiation

In Great Britain most houses are built with a pitched roof. Unfortunately these houses were built at a time when solar thermal systems were not very popular, so many of the roof directions will have a less than optimum orientation for solar energy. This effectively reduces the amount of time per day a solar collector is exposed to useful solar radiation. Where it isn't possible to install a solar collector facing the best direction, another orientation can be chosen provided the reduced exposure to solar radiation is considered. Please see fig 90 for details of this effect.

angle of inclination

Like its orientation, the angle of a solar collector will also impact on the amount of solar radiation able to strike its absorber.

The collector installation angle likely to deliver the most annual solar energy contribution in the UK starts at around 35° from horizontal for the Channel Islands and rises steadily to around 42° for the Shetland Islands north of Scotland.

Deviation from this optimum angle will cause a drop in available annual solar radiation and therefore collector energy output.

compass point and bearing			non-optimum angle and orientation factor									
ENE = 67.5	80	1.27	1.3	1.35	1.39	1.45	1.54	x	x	x	x
E	90	1.27	1.28	1.3	1.33	1.37	1.43	1.52	x	x	x
	100	1.27	1.25	1.25	1.25	1.28	1.33	1.41	1.52	x	x
ESE = 112.5	110	1.27	1.25	1.2	1.2	1.22	1.25	1.32	1.43	x	x
	120	1.27	1.2	1.16	1.15	1.16	1.19	1.25	1.35	1.47	x
	130	1.27	1.19	1.14	1.11	1.11	1.14	1.19	1.28	1.41	x
SE = 135	140	1.27	1.18	1.11	1.08	1.08	1.1	1.15	1.23	1.35	1.54
	150	1.27	1.16	1.09	1.05	1.04	1.06	1.11	1.19	1.32	1.52
SSE = 157.5	160	1.27	1.15	1.08	1.03	1.02	1.04	1.09	1.16	1.28	1.47
	170	1.27	1.14	1.06	1.02	1.01	1.02	1.06	1.15	1.27	1.47
SOUTH	180	1.27	1.14	1.06	1.02	1	1.02	1.06	1.14	1.27	1.45
	190	1.27	1.14	1.06	1.02	1	1.02	1.06	1.14	1.27	1.45
SSW = 202.5	200	1.27	1.15	1.06	1.03	1.01	1.03	1.08	1.15	1.27	1.47
	210	1.27	1.15	1.08	1.04	1.03	1.04	1.09	1.16	1.3	1.47
SW = 225	220	1.27	1.16	1.1	1.06	1.05	1.08	1.12	1.2	1.32	1.49
	230	1.27	1.18	1.12	1.09	1.09	1.11	1.16	1.23	1.37	1.54
	240	1.27	1.19	1.15	1.12	1.14	1.16	1.2	1.3	1.43	x
WSW = 247.5	250	1.27	1.22	1.18	1.18	1.18	1.22	1.28	1.37	1.49	x
	260	1.27	1.23	1.22	1.22	1.25	1.28	1.35	1.45	x	x
W	270	1.27	1.27	1.27	1.28	1.32	1.37	1.45	x	x	x
WNW = 292.5	280	1.27	1.28	1.32	1.35	1.41	1.47	x	x	x	x
		0	10	20	30	40	50	60	70	80	90
		angle of collector (0=horizontal)									

fig 90: angle of orientation factors

Note: This chart data is based on locations where the optimum collector position would be approximately south at 38° inclination (for example, central Britain; latitude 52°-54°). Charts for other latitudes would show slightly different figures.

how to use the angle and orientation factor table, fig 90

The two columns on the left show compass bearings along with compass points (for example, due west = compass bearing 270°). The row along the bottom shows the collector angle (a collector laid flat on the ground would be at zero degrees).

As an example let's consider a collector installation in central England on a roof facing south south east (SSE) and with an angle of 20° inclination from the ground:

Looking at where the SSE orientation (roughly compass bearing 160°) and the 20° angle intersect on the table, solar collectors mounted on this roof would need to be approximately 1.08 times larger than solar collectors mounted at the optimum orientation and angle in order to absorb about the same amount of energy.

Note: the table shows 'x' in some boxes; these angles/orientations have an unacceptable drop in available solar radiation and should be avoided.

shading

Wherever possible, try to avoid objects casting a shadow over solar collectors by choosing an alternative location or removing the objects (though many trees have a significant visual and environmental benefit and may be protected by law; this book doesn't advocate cutting down trees!).

If this isn't practical, an estimate of the effect of this shading should be made and the collector size adjusted where necessary.

Imagine the path of the sun across the sky at three times of the year; June, December and March (sun-path diagrams are readily available on the internet and may be useful for you) and estimate what percentage of the collector surface area will fall in shade each day.

In June the days are longer (16 to 19 hours depending on latitude), the sun will appear much higher in the sky and any trees would need to be very close to the collector to cause shade. This is the time of year when solar collectors will be delivering the most energy, so shading in summer is a major concern.

In December the days are shorter (6 to 8 hours), the sun will take a much lower path across the sky and the winter months account for a much smaller percentage of a solar collector's annual energy output (for a south facing roof about 10% of the total for December, January and February) so the effect of shading in winter will be less than at other times of year. It's also worth remembering that deciduous trees will lose their leaves in winter.

Don't be tempted to increase a collector's surface area by a large amount if shading only occurs in December and January as this extra collector size will often work out relatively expensive compared to its energy yield from winter solar radiation.

The path of the sun in March is similar to September and travels across the skyline somewhere between the June and December paths. Daylight lasts for about 12 hours and many trees will still have their leaves in September.

Once an estimate of the effect of shading has been made, multiply the collector surface area figure already calculated (after taking account of angle/orientation reductions) by:

- little or no shading (less than 20% shading)   1
- moderate shading (20 to 60% shading)   1.25
- significant shading (60 to 80% shading)   1.5
- heavy shading (more than 80% shading)   2

Note: due to the potentially significant increase in quantity or size (and thus cost) of solar collectors required it is often impractical to consider sites with heavy shading.

sizing method 1: recap

To calculate the final collector aperture surface area
multiply number of hot water users by:
- 1 m² of flat plate collector or
- 0.7 m² of evacuated tube collector
- adjust for location (see fig 89)
- adjust for orientation and angle of inclination (see fig 90)
- adjust for local shading

sizing method 2: recap

To calculate the final collector aperture surface area
- divide the dedicated solar volume (Vs) (estimated using the method described on page 129) by 30
- multiply this figure by most relevant figure from table according to collector type
- adjust for location (see fig 89)
- adjust for orientation and angle of inclination (see fig 90)
- adjust for local shading

exceptions to collector sizing methods 1 and 2

Certain solar hot water system designs require the freedom to deviate from the sizing guidelines described in methods 1 and 2.

rapid heating drainback system

In this design heat transfer medium drains out of the collector (and therefore field of solar irradiance) when the target temperature is reached in the hot water storage vessel. As there is no possibility of the fluid overheating the collector can be significantly oversized, which has the advantage of reducing the amount of time required in order to heat a given volume of stored water compared to a system where the collector is sized using method 1 or 2.

Whilst this design can deliver perfectly safe and abundant domestic hot water, its merits are not widely acknowledged by influential guide books or key regulatory documents, which may be one reason for its rarity in the UK.

In addition, it is not simply a matter of oversizing the collector; other aspects of the system design must also be considered to ensure reliable and safe operation and an installer experienced in this concept should be sought.

solar hot water system with additional heating demand

Where the design allows for the priority delivery of solar energy to hot water and for surplus energy to a swimming pool, the sizing requirements can change significantly. This would be an excellent use of surplus solar heat.

A design delivering solar energy to a space-heating circuit (radiators or underfloor heating) may also deviate from the standard sizing rules.

However, after considering the required additional investment, embodied carbon of extra components and likely solar energy benefit, it is often not worth considering a solar thermal system of this nature with a storage vessel volume (for heating support) of below 400 litres and a collector surface area of less than 6 square metres.

Where the design must make a contribution to a heating circuit as well as its main hot water function, it is not uncommon in other European countries to find storage vessel volumes of 600-2000 litres and collector arrays of 8-14 square metres in a domestic property.

Even taking the largest figures shown here, the system would only deliver a minority share of the energy required to heat a home (though there would be a greater contribution of the annual energy required to provide hot water). This is partly due to the limited solar resource available.

The greatest amount of energy to heat a typical British home is required from around September through to May, with the highest demand during December, January and February. Compare this to available solar energy, which typically peaks in June and July, and a mismatch is apparent.

regulations and system sizing

The building regulations for England and Wales now include a section (known as Part L) covering the energy efficiency of heat-generating equipment in homes (Scotland and Northern Ireland have similar regulations). The regulation itself is sufficiently vague so that more than one solution may be considered (in the hope that the regulation would not stifle innovation).

However, there is an approved supporting document to Part L called the Domestic Building Services Compliance Guide, which sets out in detail a way of meeting the minimum standards recommended to comply with the regulation. The guide covers all current forms of heat-generating appliances found in domestic buildings, and most likely system sizes, though the guide is not intended as a sizing tool.

The solar hot water section of the guide details various aspects of system design and installation, and mentions sizing in two areas:
1. there is a recommendation to allow for a loss of performance when siting collectors in shaded areas (reference is made to document SAP2009*, which attempts to quantify these losses). There is no recommendation for minimum collector surface area.
2. there is a recommendation to provide a minimum volume of stored water that can only be heated by solar energy, and two options are given:
   a) 25 litres of stored water per net square metre of collector absorber area or
   b) a dedicated solar volume (or equivalent heat capacity) of at least 80% of daily hot water demand (as defined in SAP2009*)

*SAP2005 is the UK government's Standard Assessment Procedure (SAP) for energy rating of buildings. It covers all types of energy losses and energy gains and is a method of scoring and comparing the energy efficiency of buildings – it is not a design tool but can be used as a basic way to assess the energy contribution of a relatively simple solar hot water system design. SAP is intended to be reviewed every few years.

The guide provides useful details on certain minimum requirements relating to solar hot water systems, however it should be noted that the guide is neither a statutory requirement (other methods may be considered to achieve compliance with the regulation) or a sizing tool (it is not intended to determine whether a system will offer value for money, or provide a gross energy benefit that meets the design requirements or site conditions). It is also worth pointing out that the guide is expected to evolve with technological advances; future revisions may alter what we now believe to be good practice and may address areas of concern within the current version of the guide.

whole systems

Solar thermal systems for domestic hot water can be configured in many ways and with varying degrees of complexity and effectiveness. Here are a few designs.

thermosiphon solar circulation in an open-vented system with indirect heat exchange to stored water

This system consists of one or more solar collectors connected (often coupled closely) to a hot water storage vessel. The heat transfer medium is dedicated to the solar pipe circuit (it is not the water that ultimately passes through distribution pipes to hot water taps and other outlets). In climates with frost risk, the heat transfer medium is an antifreeze solution.

The heat transfer medium is moved from the collector to the store by gravity circulation – there is no pump or controller.

The collector remains filled with heat transfer medium at all times and the solar pipe circuit may be open vented (operating at atmospheric pressure; as shown in fig 91) or sealed and pressurised (above atmospheric pressure).

characteristics

- as the collector must be below the level of the storage vessel, the choice of installation location for system components is rather limited.
- where the collector and storage vessel are close coupled and the storage vessel must be installed outside the building, there is a risk of frost rupturing the storage vessel (only the heat transfer medium in the solar pipe circuit contains an antifreeze solution).

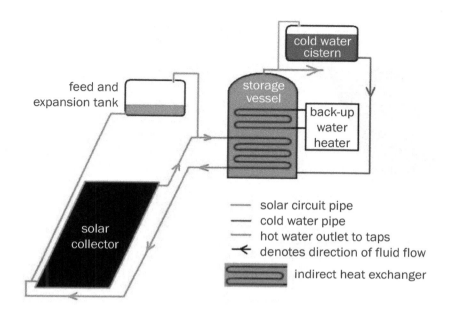

fig 91: thermosiphon solar circulation system

- with very few components and no electricity consumption, the design is simple, reliable (when installed in an appropriate climate) and often inexpensive.
- to prevent the potential risk of scalding hot water at taps and other outlets, an additional mixing valve must be used. This is because the design does not employ a controller and therefore cannot limit the energy contribution from solar.
- some designs feature a storage vessel mounted directly above the collector and outside the building they are serving. This can increase heat loss in exposed locations due to the cooling effect of wind passing over the storage vessel.

forced solar circulation in an open vented system with direct heat transfer to stored water

A system where the solar collector is mounted remotely from, and often above, the level of the storage vessel, requiring the system to force the heat transfer medium to circulate by using a pump.

The heat transfer medium is the same pure water that passes through to taps and other hot water outlets and no antifreeze solution is used.

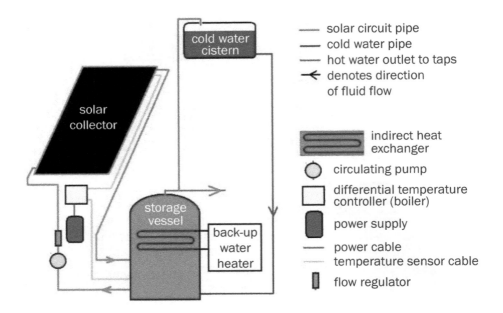

fig 92: forced solar circulation system with direct heat transfer

A source of electricity is required to power the circulating pump and there may also be some form of controller. The collector remains filled with heat transfer medium at all times and the system is not pressurised.

characteristics

- the heat transfer medium is pure water; water has a greater heat capacity than antifreeze (it can carry slightly more heat from collector to storage vessel).
- as the system uses a circulating pump, there must be a power source. This can be grid-connected 240 volt electricity or a stand-alone 12 volt supply such as from a battery or photovoltaic cell.
- use of a circulating pump allows greater flexibility when siting the collector.
- being unable to use antifreeze solution as a heat transfer medium means this design is unsuitable for use in locations susceptible to frost, or during seasons when frost may occur unless an equally adequate means of frost protection can be provided for all foreseeable circumstances. Options available include frost-resistant pipes, automatic drain down (a temperature-controlled valve opens and dumps water within the collector) and stored-heat frost protection (the system controller detects near-zero temperature in the collector and activates forced circulation). Heat from the storage vessel warms the collector briefly, and the process is repeated as required until the collector temperature exceeds +4°C.

Note: this method assumes a differential temperature controller is installed, sufficient heat is available in the storage vessel when required and the system has an uninterruptible power source (in the event of power cuts).

- to prevent the potential risk of scalding hot water at taps and other outlets, an additional mixing valve may be used, or deactivation of the circulating pump by a differential temperature controller with suitable maximum storage vessel temperature limit (such as 60°C).
- as the process of consuming hot water requires the replenishment of heat transfer medium to the collector with pure water (which contains a fresh supply of minerals), it is strongly recommended to use a water softening or conditioning device in hard water areas thereby preventing limescale from clogging pipes in and adjacent to the collector.

forced solar circulation in an open vented system with indirect heat transfer to stored water

In this system the solar collector is mounted remotely and often above the level of the storage vessel, requiring the system to force the heat transfer medium to circulate using a pump.

The heat transfer medium is a separate fluid from that distributed to taps and other hot water outlets, therefore an antifreeze solution is likely to be used.

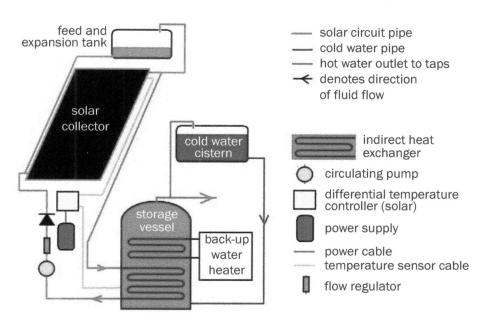

fig 93: forced solar circulation system with indirect heat transfer

A source of electricity is required to power the circulating pump and there may also be some form of controller.

The collector remains filled with heat transfer medium at all times and the system is not pressurised above atmospheric pressure.

Heat from the collector is transferred to the storage vessel by means of an internal coil or external plate heat exchanger. To prevent uncontrolled and unwanted movement of heat from the storage vessel to the collector at night (by gravity circulation) at least one check valve is installed in the solar transmission pipes.

characteristics

- the heat transfer medium is likely to be a mixture of water and antifreeze; this has a slightly smaller heat capacity than pure water.
- as the system uses a circulating pump, there must be a power source. This can be grid-connected 240 volt electricity or a stand-alone 12 volt supply such as from a battery or photovoltaic cell.
- use of a circulating pump allows greater flexibility when siting the collector.
- the design is suitable for use in locations prone to frost provided the heat transfer medium contains sufficient antifreeze to protect external components in all foreseeable circumstances. The use of antifreeze removes the need for frost-resistant pipes, automatic drain down devices, the export of stored heat or an uninterruptible power source.
- to prevent the potential risk of scalding hot water at taps and other outlets, an additional mixing valve may be used, or deactivation of the circulating pump by a controller with suitable maximum storage vessel temperature limit (such as 60°C).
- as the heat transfer medium is part of an open vented system, there is the possibility that evaporation of some antifreeze may occur during periods of high solar irradiance, and it is important to periodically check the water-antifreeze ratio and top-up in the correct proportions as required.
- in this design, heat transfer medium is not regularly replaced by pure water, therefore limescale within the collector and transmission pipes will not be a concern.

forced solar circulation in a fully-filled, sealed and pressurised system with indirect heat exchange to stored water

In this system the solar collector is mounted remotely and often above the level of the storage vessel, requiring the system to force heat transfer medium to circulate using a pump.

The heat transfer medium is a separate fluid from that distributed to taps and other hot water outlets therefore an antifreeze solution is likely to be used.

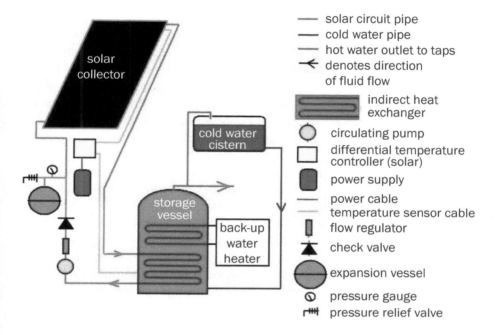

fig 94: forced solar circulation system, fully sealed and pressurised with indirect heat exchange

A source of electricity is required to power the circulating pump and there will be some form of controller.

The collector remains filled with heat transfer medium at all times and the system is pressurised to operate between 1 and 4 bar above atmospheric pressure (depending on components and operating conditions).

Heat from the collector is transferred to the storage vessel by means of an internal coil or external-plate heat exchanger. Some designs feature a small heat exchange device designed to replace the electric immersion heater in an existing hot water cylinder. This is often referred to as a 'hot rod' and due to its limited heat exchange capacity and relative position in the cylinder may deliver unsatisfactory results.

To prevent uncontrolled and unwanted movement of heat from storage vessel to collector at night (by gravity circulation), at least one check valve is installed in the solar transmission pipes.

characteristics
- the heat transfer medium is likely to be a mixture of water and antifreeze; this has a slightly smaller heat capacity than pure water.
- as the system uses a circulating pump, there must be a power source. This can be grid-connected 240 volt electricity or a stand-alone 12 volt supply such as from a battery or photovoltaic cell.
- the use of a circulating pump allows greater flexibility when siting the collector.
- the design is suitable for use in locations prone to frost, provided the heat transfer medium contains sufficient antifreeze to protect external components in all foreseeable circumstances. The use of antifreeze removes the need for frost-resistant pipes, automatic drain down devices, the export of stored heat or an uninterruptible power source.
- to prevent the potential risk of scalding hot water at taps and other outlets, an additional mixing valve may be used, or alternatively excess solar heat contribution can be halted through deactivation of the circulating pump by a differential temperature controller with suitable maximum storage vessel temperature limit (such as 60°C).
- as the heat transfer medium is part of a sealed and pressurised hydraulic circuit, there is no opportunity for antifreeze to evaporate. In the event of high solar irradiance and low hot water demand, heat transfer medium may be lost following expansion which causes excess pressure, via a pressure relief valve, although this can often be avoided by providing a generous expansion vessel capacity.
- in this design, heat transfer medium is not regularly replaced by pure water, therefore limescale within the collector and transmission pipes will not be a concern.

forced solar circulation in a sealed or open-vented drainback system with indirect heat exchange to stored water

In this system the solar collector is mounted remotely and above the level of the storage vessel, requiring the system to force heat transfer medium to circulate using a pump.

The heat transfer medium is a separate fluid from that distributed to taps and other hot water outlets, therefore an antifreeze solution may be used.

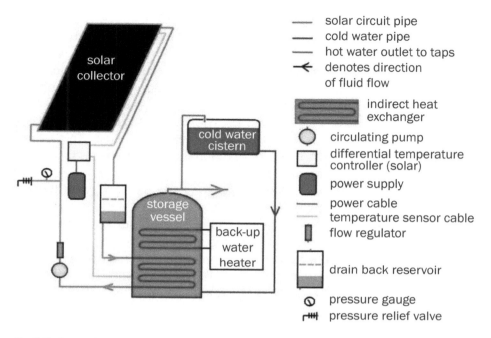

solar collector

cold water cistern

storage vessel

back-up water heater

——	solar circuit pipe
——	cold water pipe
——	hot water outlet to taps
—◄	denotes direction of fluid flow
	indirect heat exchanger
○	circulating pump
□	differential temperature controller (solar)
	power supply
——	power cable
------	temperature sensor cable
	flow regulator
	drain back reservoir
◔	pressure gauge
⊢Ш	pressure relief valve

fig 95: forced solar circulation in a sealed drainback system with indirect heat exchange

A source of electricity is required to power the circulating pump and there will be some form of controller.

The collector only fills with heat transfer medium when forced circulation is activated, and at all other times contains a pocket of air.

The system may be open vented or sealed (depending on system design – fig 95 shows a sealed system).

Heat from the collector is transferred to the storage vessel by means of an internal coil or external-plate heat exchanger.

characteristics

- the heat transfer medium may be pure water (a separate sealed volume of water from that distributed to taps and other hot water outlets) or a mixture of water and antifreeze (this has a slightly smaller heat capacity than pure water).

- as the system uses a circulating pump, there must be a power source.

This can be grid-connected 240 volt electricity or a stand-alone 12 volt supply such as from a battery or photovoltaic cell (12 volt versions are not common).

- the use of a circulating pump allows greater flexibility when siting the collector but the system design demands a minimum fall angle on all transmission pipes from collector to drainback reservoir in order to ensure heat transfer medium can freely drain out of the collector and frost-prone pipes when forced circulation is deactivated. This often restricts the siting of the collector and drainback reservoir and may not be practical for some properties.
- many drainback systems utilise a circulating pump with an impeller (as opposed to a diaphragm pump). Therefore, the pump must be installed lower than the drainback reservoir and must have sufficient power to force the heat transfer medium upwards to the collectors.
- the design is suitable for use in locations prone to frost, provided the heat transfer medium can completely drain from all exposed components or contains sufficient antifreeze to protect external components in all foreseeable circumstances. The use of either method removes the need for frost-resistant pipes, the export of stored heat or an uninterruptible power source.
- to prevent the potential risk of scalding hot water at taps and other outlets an additional mixing valve may be used, or deactivation of the circulating pump by a differential temperature controller with suitable maximum storage vessel temperature limit (such as 60°C).
- in the event of high solar irradiance and low hot water demand, heat transfer medium will not be present in the collector and so there is no opportunity for antifreeze (if used) to vaporise *provided* the system controller has a maximum collector temperature function activated.
- where the hydraulic circuit is sealed, there is no opportunity for the heat transfer medium to evaporate, removing the need for regular fluid top-ups.
- as the system relies on the permanent presence of an air pocket automatic air release devices are not required.
- in this design heat transfer medium is not regularly replaced and limescale within the collector and transmission pipes will not be a concern.

integration of solar and backup water heater

In order to get the very best out of a solar thermal system for hot water, it is important to ensure that it is correctly integrated with the backup water heater. Solar energy should be allowed to pass from the solar collectors to the household hot water outlets in a way that reduces the contribution of backup heat and prevents harm to users or backup water heaters caused by excessive water temperatures.

Where the backup water heater is an electric immersion heater or fossil-fuelled system boiler, this would be achieved by the use of:
- **time control** to prevent the backup water heater from contributing heat during daylight hours when solar energy could be available. Without this control, the backup water heater would add fossil-fuel derived heat faster (even in strong sunlight) and displace the solar contribution.
- **temperature control** to ensure the backup water heater only adds as much energy as is needed to heat water to the desired temperature. Without this control, the backup water heater would consume fossil fuel unnecessarily and overheat the water.

Where the backup water heater is a boiler, and the energy is transferred by pipes connected to a heat exchanger, fossil fuel can be further saved by 'boiler interlock'. This is not a product but an arrangement of controls and valves that prevents the boiler switching on unnecessarily.

Boiler interlock allows the control of when the boiler is switched off and circulation of its heat transfer fluid to be stopped, until further heat is required, to be determined by the temperature measured at the hot water vessel.

A boiler without 'boiler interlock' is controlled by a temperature measured in a location *other than* the hot water storage vessel. It could be the pipe returning circulated liquid to the boiler for futher heating, and this is a much less effective means of controlling boiler fuel consumption.

Where the backup water heater is a combination boiler ('combi boiler') or instantaneous water heater, this would be achieved by the use of:
- **temperature control** as above (time control is not required for a water heater that only delivers heat as hot water is demanded). Some backup water heaters are not designed to accept solar preheated water and cannot sufficiently reduce their heat contribution as preheated water is passed through the heater. This can result in wasteful and dangerous hot water temperatures at outlets and premature failure of components within the backup water heater.

maintenance

There are very few moving parts in a solar hot water system. Nevertheless, these and other elements of the system will need occasional inspection and maintenance.

Frequency of maintenance depends on the system type and should follow recommendations from component manufacturers and the system installer.

It is common for a professionally installed system to have a maintenance interval of between 1 and 5 years (depending on system type), with a partial service to check the operation of safety-related components, fluid circulation and pressure, and frost protection measures at least.

A comprehensive service might additionally check the condition of collectors, collector fixings, transmission pipes and cables, insulation materials, storage vessel and heat exchanger condition and may also include the replacement of antifreeze-based heat transfer medium if required.

A sample maintenance checklist is shown in the *appendix*, see page 258.

permissions

planning consent

In 2007 the planning regulations for England and Wales (slightly different regulations apply to Scotland and Northern Ireland) relating to solar equipment in houses was a matter of interpretation.

Some elements of planning guidance seemed to strongly support the installation of solar collectors (particularly on new houses) and others were sufficiently vague that individual planning authorities seemed unsure as to the most appropriate advice for those asking for consent.

This difference in interpretation occasionally led to similar houses in neighbouring districts to be dealt with in opposing ways; one district would clearly state that consent was not needed and the other would require its residents to submit an application for consideration (for which a fee would be payable).

This seemed a little unfair, but since April 2008 the newly revised General Permitted Development Order (part of the Town and Country Planning Act) has removed much of the 'red tape' and resolved matters in favour of those wishing to install solar thermal systems on their homes.

District planning authorities are now stating on websites or information leaflets that formal planning consent for solar thermal systems on domestic buildings is not required, though there are some conditions and exceptions:

- **listed buildings** these buildings are protected by law usually for their architectural / historic value and a formal application for listed building consent would be required where solar collectors are to be installed, though this doesn't necessarily mean consent would be refused.

- **buildings within areas of outstanding natural beauty, conservation areas, world heritage sites or national parks** special conditions may apply and a formal planning application would probably be required, though may not necessarily be refused (particularly if the solar collectors cannot easily be seen).

It's worth mentioning that a building does not actually need to be within the boundaries of the protected area as national park authorities may have planning jurisdiction over buildings that can be seen from the boundaries of the protected area.

- **buildings where solar collectors protrude significantly beyond the existing structure.** This would certainly apply to solar collectors installed in such a way that they visually alter the external shape of the building; for example, solar collectors mounted on an inclined frame attached to a flat roof or wall, or collectors projecting above the existing ridgeline of a roof, or protruding more than 200mm from the building's roof or wall surface.

- **buildings where solar collectors are installed on a free-standing frame or other structure not attached to the building.** In this case, there is a limit to the size of collector array allowed without the need for planning permission of 9 square metres.

In the general permitted development order rules, there is also an additional requirement for solar collectors to be installed onto a building in such a way that they do not, wherever practical, have a negative impact on the visual appeal of the building.

This is the only significantly vague aspect of the new rules, and could perhaps be interpreted in a way that restricts the installation of solar collectors.

However, I would like to think that planning authorities will enter into the spirit of government green policy, and encourage solar collector installations without unnecessary red tape.

The key words in this stipulation are 'wherever practical' as this suggests that a solar collector installation allowed under the terms of the general permitted development order but with the exception of this visual appeal clause (for example, the ideal roof for collectors is south facing but it is clearly visible from the public highway), should be permitted where it can be shown to be impractical to position the solar collectors on any other part of the building (for example, an unacceptable performance drop from collectors installed on an alternative north-facing roof).

If in doubt, ask your planning authority.

building regulations

The Building Regulations for England and Wales (and associated approved documents) set out the minimum requirements for construction work undertaken in domestic properties, and are designed to ensure the completed work is safe and energy efficient. They include guidance on alterations to 'controlled services or fittings' of which a hot water storage vessel is one.

In 2011, the UK government department responsible for the building regulations modified its guidelines relating to the notification of certain types of building work. The previous guidelines made a requirement for all new hot water cylinders to be formally notified under the building regulations by either:
a) inspection and approval by the local building control officer, or
b) installation, testing and self-certification by a trained and registered competent person, for example a hot water cylinder installer approved by a government-recognised competent persons scheme.

The revised guidelines now require solar hot water systems, in addition to the hot water cylinder itself, to also be notified by a solar trained and registered competent person or a local building control officer. This extra requirement makes it a bit more complex and bureaucratic to install your own solar hot water system, but not impossible.

To find an approved qualified installer, consult a reputable trade association whose members subscribe to a government recognised 'competent person scheme', see *resources*, page 263 for details of trade associations and competent person schemes).

The building regulations also set out requirements concerning the safety of structural alterations, resistance to the spread of fire, and modifications to combustion heating appliances – all of which could form part of work associated with installing a domestic solar thermal system.

Note: following the establishment of devolved governments for Wales, Northern Ireland and Scotland (and perhaps in future, regional devolved governments in England), the building regulations for England may be different for these parts of the UK. A similar situation may also apply to the Isle of Man and the Channel Isles; if in any doubt, consult a representative of the building inspectorate for your location.

financial incentives

For some years now there have been a variety of incentives designed to entice residents to invest in solar hot water technology for their home.

These incentives began with the Clear Skies initiative, covering England and Wales, and offered by other UK devolved governments with some minor alterations. The scheme was largely successful due to the simplicity of the application process for residents and the low cost of participation for competent installers. Successful applicants were able to claim a £500 cash-back grant on completion and payment of a solar hot water installation to acceptable standards by an approved installer.

This scheme was replaced by the Low Carbon Buildings Programme, a revised version of the original scheme with greater emphasis on safeguards for residents.

Unfortunately the replacement scheme was less successful, due partly to significant changes in the requirements for participating installers and product manufacturers and a reduction in the cash-back grant value to £400. Many previously participating installers chose not to support the scheme and applications from residents for the lower grant amount dropped.

Alongside these schemes was an assortment of district and regional incentives. Forward-thinking local authorities came up with a variety of funding options for their residents, from top-up grants of up to £1000 to schemes offering interest-free loans, allowing residents to pay for an installation over the life of the system. Some of these local schemes continue today so it is well worth contacting your local authority to check on developments.

In addition, there are plans to introduce a new scheme in October 2012 in many parts of the UK. The Renewable Heat Incentive (RHI) is a scheme which aims to encourage the uptake of heat-producing small-scale renewable energy installations by offering a regular payment for the heat energy generated.

At the time of writing, the details are very sketchy but solar hot water systems may attract a figure of around 18 pence for every kilowatt hour of heat energy generated, even though that energy is subsequently consumed in the same property.

This would be a significant shift from flat rate cash-back grants to a much fairer pay-as-you-generate incentive.

The scheme is still in its infancy and following a change of government in 2010, there is talk of another scheme the 'Green Deal' which could impact the deployment of RHI; so much of the devilish detail could change!

For the latest information, check the web pages of the relevant government department responsible for energy in your location, or search for 'Renewable Heat Incentive'.

preparing to install

The following chapters are intended as a practical guide to successfully installing the various elements of one of the domestic solar hot water systems better suited to DIY and demonstrated on LILI residential weekend courses.

If you intend to use parts of this information with other components, you should check first with the component supplier to ensure compatibility.

The guide contains detailed sections showing how the main parts should fit together in the whole system design.

Due to the variety of configurations, existing heating and hot water products and circumstances found in domestic properties throughout the UK, the guide should not be considered comprehensive.

This system is based on an indirect fully-filled pressurised design and is intended for use in homes with a vented hot water system connected to an indirect gas, LPG, wood or oil boiler, or direct electric immersion heater. Subject to minor adjustments in system design and product specification, the system would also be suitable for homes with an unvented hot water cylinder or a thermal store. It is a system design with components and methods carefully selected to achieve a good balance between cost, availability of materials, ease of installation and durability. However, it is not the only design and you may wish to consider alternatives described elsewhere in this book.

The use of this design does not necessarily ensure compliance with local building regulations or codes, which vary from location to location and are amended from time to time.

The key components are:
- 2 or 3 solar collectors made by Sundwel solar (Atlas) or WATT (type 3000)
- a vented solar hot water cylinder of the single coil preheat or twin coil type
- a central heating or boiler circulating pump with 1in hydraulic connections
- a high temperature non-return valve
- a flow regulator with 2-8 litres per minute adjustment range

- an 18 Litre (2 Atlas) 24 Litre (3 Atlas or 2 WATT) or 35 Litre (3 WATT) expansion vessel with a 3.5 bar or higher working pressure
- a 3 bar pressure relief valve and pressure gauge with a 0-4 or 0-10 bar display range
- a RESOL AX differential temperature controller (DTC) with 2 temperature sensors
- various isolating valves (some are required to withstand high temperature)
- a container for capturing discharged heat transfer medium
- high temperature pipe, fittings and insulation

general notes

There are a number of things that should be observed for a reasonably trouble-free installation.
- some components specify a particular direction of water flow and it is wise when assembling to first check for direction of flow arrows on the body of the components.
- care should be taken when tightening the nuts on plumbing fittings. Gripping components too tightly can damage them internally; a vice should *not* be used for this task.
- plan the task before picking up any tools, and it may help in the event of troubleshooting to note down existing pipe and cable configurations before making alterations.
- don't try to install alone. Consider forming a small team of 'solar self-builders' to share each others installation work. Apart from the safety risks of working alone, you will make the job harder and less enjoyable than it should be.

Make good use of the information provided and available. Read the manuals supplied with components carefully, and if you've attended one of our courses remember you can contact us if you have questions.

health and safety

The installation of solar heating components involves working with a range of potentially hazardous materials and equipment, and working in potentially dangerous locations. Carefully consider the risks to you and others when installing components around your home; health and safety should be the top priority.

Top tips for accident prevention include:
- think about the hazards, the likelihood and severity of things going wrong, and who it would affect. An indication of typical hazards, risks and measures to control them are listed in the *appendix,* page 260.
- don't work alone, especially where the work involves moving heavy or awkward objects, or working in confined spaces or at height.
- remove combustible materials when using naked flames.
- ensure working areas are well lit; potential hazards first need to be visible!
- wear suitable personal protective equipment (PPE) if required; safety helmet, goggles, gloves, overalls, safety shoes, ear defenders.
- choose the right tools for each task.

tools

Here is a list of tools and consumables you may need:
- blowtorch, solder and flux
- fine abrasive pad or wire wool
- soldering mat and *powder* fire extinguisher (a precaution when soldering)
- adjustable spanners
- adjustable pliers
- screwdrivers
- tape measure
- wood saw, hacksaw and junior hacksaw
- pipe cutters
- pipe benders
- scissors and retractable knife
- inspection lamp (for working in lofts or dark areas) and torch
- PTFE tape and Jointing compound
- spirit level
- power drill
- masonry drill bits (for fixing and passing pipes through roof / walls)
- metal drill bits (for drilling collector straps and rails)
- chalk (for temporary marking on roof)
- pointing trowel (to help slide roof tiles up and down)
- access equipment (scaffold tower, etc.)
- dust mask (for working in lofts) and protective workwear
- cable cutters
- claw hammer
- cable ties, cable clips and electrical tape
- silicone sealant and decorators caulk (gap filler)

- wall plugs, screws and nails
- copper or brass fittings and pipe (for minor pipework alterations from your existing boiler to your new solar hot water cylinder)
- hose pipe and hose clip (for draining away fluids)
- stepladder
- bucket and some rags (to catch minor fluid leaks, etc.)
- hand trolley (for moving heavy objects)

pipes, fittings and insulation

Things to consider when choosing the route for your pipes:
- if possible try to ensure your pipes maintain a steady upward path from the lowest to highest points in the system. This will avoid the possibility of large pockets of trapped air when filling the system with fluid and make draining easier.

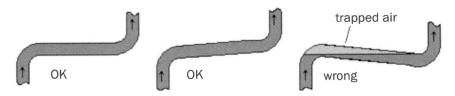

fig 96: pipe paths

- try to avoid lots of tight bends as these will increase fluid flow resistance
- allow enough working space around pipes for tightening and soldering joints
- remember to allow space around pipes for insulation
- keep pipe runs between solar collectors and hot water cylinder short wherever possible as this will reduce potential heat loss

When drilling holes:
- check first for hidden cables and pipes in walls and floors
- ensure any holes that must be made in structural timber do not affect their load-bearing properties. If in doubt, there are many good DIY manuals you can use, or contact a professional for advice.

After deciding the route for your pipes, lay your pipes, pipe clips, fittings and cables out (see *electrics and wiring*, page 217 for further details) as a 'dry run' to ensure everything fits. You should use sufficient pipe clips to hold the pipework in its intended position, without the pipes being able to sag.

fig 97: an insulated pipe in situ

Fig 97 shows an insulated pipe clipped at regular intervals with copper saddle bands over the insulation. This has the advantage of reducing the amount of heat loss through splits in pipe insulation and heat conducted by the metal bands.

When installing pipes that pass from one room or compartment to another, mark the pipe ends with coloured tape as they are passed through the wall or floor. This will:
• prevent accidentally connecting pipes the wrong way round
• avoid debris from entering the pipe ends and causing a blockage

Inspect all pipes and fittings closely before using them; you may discover that damage has occurred that would cause a leak.

bending copper pipe

There are two main methods to bend copper pipe; handheld pipe benders (complete with guides) or a hand bending spring. You can use either but you will generally get more accurate results from the handheld pipe benders shown here.

fig 98: hand benders with metal guide

fig 99: pencil mark the pipe where you want to make a bend

fig 100: place the pipe in the hand benders, slide in the bending guide and align the pencil mark

A small, straight piece of copper pipe with an evenly cut end can be placed in the forming channel of the hand bender at right angles to, and centred on, the pencil mark.

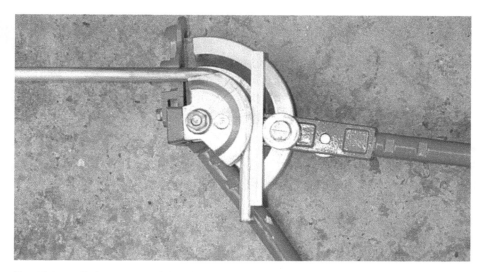

fig 101: pull the arms of the hand bender together until a 90° bend is achieved

If you are unsure of the accuracy of the bend, remove the section of pipe and lay it over a table corner or similar object with a known right angle. If the bend angle is too small, replace the pipe into the hand bender and complete the bend. If the angle is too large, try carefully pulling the bend out a little by hand, or start again with a new piece of pipe.

joining

The joining of pipes and fittings may involve one or more of the methods shown here.

compression

A compression fitting uses a brass nut to squeeze an 'olive' around the piece of copper pipe to be connected.

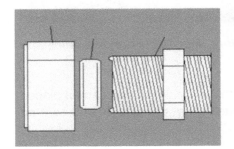 

fig 102: an isolating valve with compression ends

A small amount of jointing compound or polytetrafluoroethylene (PTFE) tape is sometimes applied between the mating surfaces of the olive and fitting to ensure a watertight joint, though this is more a personal preference than an absolute must.

soldering

Solder fittings must be heated and a quantity of solder melted in between the pipe and fitting to create a permanent watertight seal.

Solder comes in a variety of compositions:
leaded

Suitable for pipes and fittings carrying domestic liquids not intended for human consumption (non-potable water, central heating system liquids), leaded solder melts at a relatively low temperature and so should not be used on pipes carrying solar heat transfer fluids.

lead-free

Suitable for pipes and fittings that carry potable water and non-potable water or liquids, lead-free solder has a higher melting point than leaded solder, and can be used on some pipes carrying solar heat transfer fluids, which includes most systems based upon flat plate solar collectors and exposed to UK solar irradiance levels. Lead-free solder may de-solder if used in close proximity to certain high performance evacuated tube solar collectors.

silver solder / light brazing rods

The exact composition of the silver solder of light brazing rods will determine the melting point and subsequent suitability for use in solar hot water system pipes. There are two main disadvantages with using this type of solder: cost and limited fluidity (the ability to melt and run easily into fittings).

The typical steps to a successfully soldered joint are:
- clean the outer end of the pipe and inside the fitting end with a light abrasive pad or wire wool
- apply a small amount of flux to the pipe outer end (not inside the fitting as flux is corrosive to copper and can make antifreeze acidic) and push the mating surfaces together
- heat the area and feed the melted solder between the mating surfaces until a ring of solder fills the gap
- allow the joint to cool before wiping off excess flux

When soldering remember:
- remove any plastic or rubber parts from fittings before applying heat.
- solder will move towards the heat. This allows solder to run upwards into a fitting attached to a vertical pipe.
- heat will conduct quickly across copper pipe, and linger for several minutes, so handle with care and ensure recently soldered pipes and fittings are completely cool before leaving unattended.
- heat conducting through copper pipe will prefer to move upwards. Solder the lowest part of a fitting first as the rising heat will preheat the upper part and save on blow torch gas. It will also prevent accidental de-soldering.
- flux has a limited exposure to blow torch heat; too much exposure will burn off the flux and prevent solder from running into and around the fitting.

fig 103: a typical solder TEE fitting

threaded joints

A BSP threaded joint comprises a male threaded fitting that screws into a female threaded fitting, sometimes squeezing a washer or gasket between two flat ends.

This type of joint requires either:
• PTFE sealing tape bound tightly around the male thread with a small amount of jointing compound on top, or
• jointing compound applied to the male thread with hemp fibre added *or*
• a washer or gasket between the mating surfaces

fig 104: a typical threaded fitting using PTFE tape on the thread

When using PTFE tape on threaded joints, wind the tape onto the thread in a combination of flat rotations followed by twisted diagonal rotations and further flat rotations. Before screwing the fitting together, press the PTFE tape firmly into the thread and lightly lubricate the thread's leading edge. When applying PTFE tape to this type of joint, it is a good idea to both follow the course of the thread and occasionally cross the thread diagonally to increase the chance of a good, watertight seal.

plastic pipes and fittings

As a general rule, plastic pipes and fittings should *not* be used on any part of the system that will be in contact with solar heat transfer fluid. They are highly likely to melt! Please see the *pipe connections for solar collectors* section on page 49.

installing collectors

Installing solar collectors onto a roof involves a range of risks that you should be aware of and assess before starting. These include (but are not limited to):

- working at height
- manual lifting and handling (a single Atlas solar collector weighs 27kg dry; a single Type 3000 collector weighs 37kg dry)
- use of power tools
- possible fragile surfaces
- hot surfaces (such as collector pipework on sunny days)
- falling objects (such as tools from a high working platform)
- hazardous weather conditions (wind, snow, ice, rain, exposure to strong sun)
- All of these risks can be safely controlled provided you are sensible, realistic and patient. A range of hazards, risks and control measures are shown in the *appendix*, see page 260.

If in any doubt, you should seek professional advice and assistance.

how to get onto the roof

Most roof installation work can be accessed using a mobile platform tower, widely available from tool hire centres. Alternatively, you can arrange for the erection of steel scaffolding from a registered company. Whichever option is chosen it should be fit for purpose and not overloaded.

fig 105: mobile platform scaffolding tower

before going on a roof

Take a good look at the condition of the roof from underneath. The structural elements should be in good order, showing no significant signs of weakening from rot, woodworm, splitting or any other damage.

The secondary roof covering (roof felt or membrane) can be inspected for signs of holes and ageing (felt becomes very brittle after many years). If you discover that elements of the roof need repair it is wise to undertake this work before installing solar collectors.

where and how to fix the collectors

When deciding where on a roof to fix collectors, consider the following:
- try to keep the collectors close to the hot water cylinder location; this will reduce the length of pipework and heat losses from it
- minimise the potential shading from trees and buildings
- the location and condition of timber rafters onto which you will attach the collectors
- the space you will need for the number of collectors;
    each Atlas collector measures around 1.7 metres high by 90cm wide by 10cm deep *plus* mountings and any necessary gaps for hydraulic connections
    each Type 3000 collector measures around 2 metres high by 1 metre wide by 9cm deep *plus* mountings and any necessary gaps for hydraulic connections
- where you intend to penetrate the roof covering for pipes

In order to maximise system efficiency, try to position collectors as close as possible to the optimum angle and orientation and try to avoid shading from adjacent structures.

Once you have decided roughly where the collectors will be fixed, remove some tiles and have a closer look at the timbers you will a) fix the collectors to and b) avoid with fluid-carrying pipes. Consider also the other obstacles inside a roof that may cause a problem, such as cold water storage cisterns or loft space television aerials.

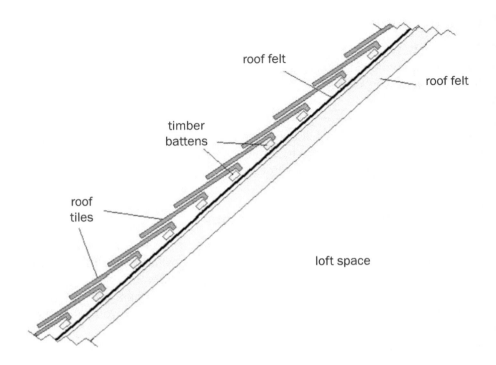

roof felt

roof felt

timber
battens

roof
tiles

loft space

fig 106: cross-section of a typical roof structure

Every roof is slightly different. Most will have a cross-section similar to fig 106 but the number of rows and columns of roof tiles and timber battens can vary greatly.

Fig 107 shows the timber layout of a typical roof (tiles and felt removed); rafters are structural and can be used for fixing of collectors; tile battens are not structural and should be avoided. It is a good idea to locate the rafters and then mark their positions on top of the felt.

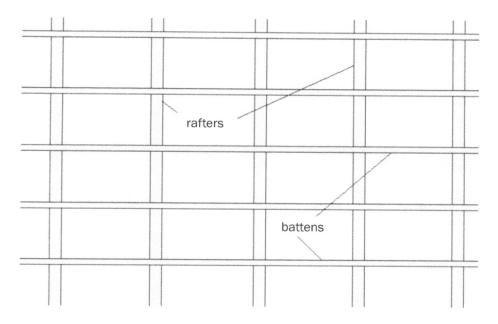

fig 107: the timber layout of a typical roof

method 1: alloy straps on a pitched roof

Many roof tiles have a cross-section with one or more peaks and valleys and it is far easier to position straps in the valley of a tile (see fig 108) than a section that is not as flat; this will help the roof tiles to fit together better once you have finished fixing the solar collectors.

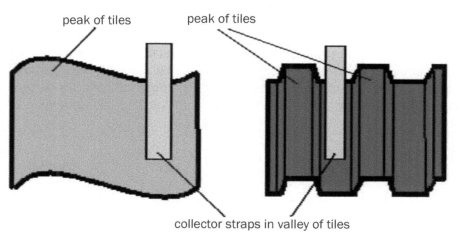

fig 108: recommended collector strap position

Ideally, one end of each strap should be attached using coach screws directly to rafters but tile profiles and rafter spacing may prevent this.

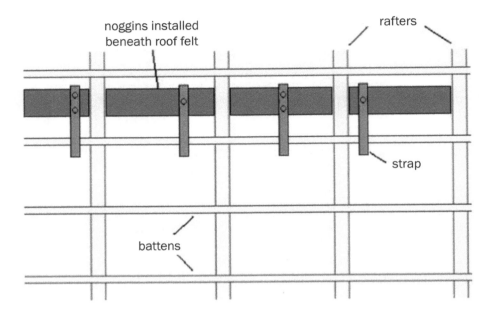

noggins installed
beneath roof felt

rafters

strap

battens

fig 109: noggins secured between rafters beneath the roof felt can form new structural timbers allowing fixing of straps with coach screws

Alternatively, a collector mounting batten (which is not the same as a roof tile batten) can be installed above the roof felt to allow you to position straps in the valley of roof tiles as direct alignment of the two is no longer essential.

A collector mounting batten is essentially a length of weather-resistant timber that is sized to fit between roof tile battens (for example, a collector batten could be tannalised timber 100mm wide by 20mm deep by a length suitable for the size of the collectors used). The depth of collector battens will be restricted by the air gap between roof felt and the underside of roof tiles.

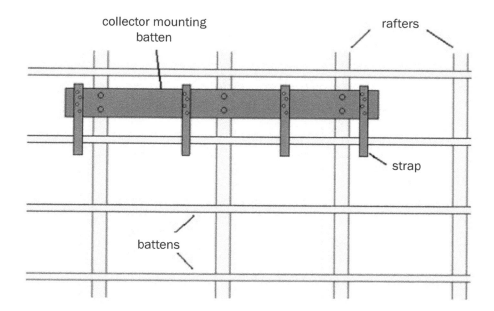

fig 110: collector mounting batten in situ

Fig 111, page 178, shows a typical pitched roof fixing for a 2 collector system: the approximate roof penetration position for the flow pipes are indicated by **A** and **B** indicates the return pipes.

Each strap should be secured to the mounting batten using sturdy roof screws (but make sure they are short enough to avoid piercing the roofing felt) and shape the end of the strap to form a hook over the timber.

Each collector should have 4 straps attached, 2 per rail. Straps should be kept short and positioned as closely to the corners of each collector as the roof tile profiles allow.

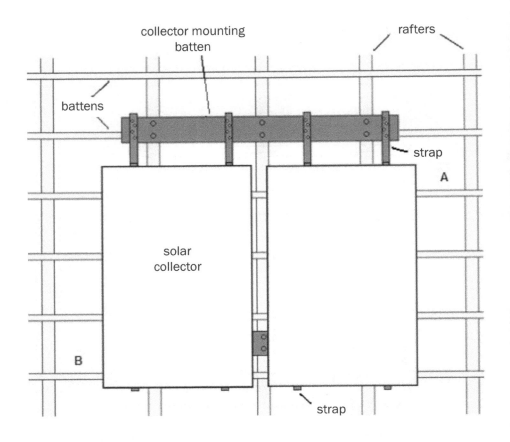

fig 111: fixing for a typical pitched roof

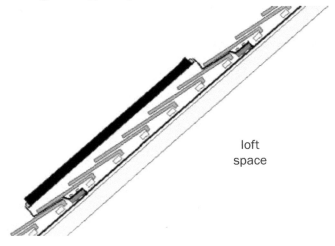

fig 112: profiles for straps (mounting battens shown)

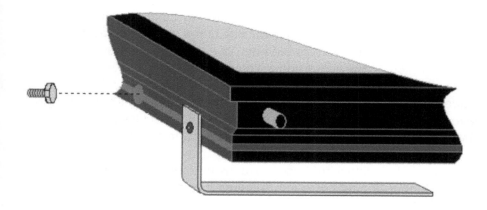

fig 113: fitting a mounting strap using built-in slotted channel

Fig 113 shows how an alloy strap is fitted to a collector via the built-in slotted channel (Atlas collector shown). The head of the set screw is inserted in the slot and slid along to align with the strap. The strap is then secured using the nut, washer and spring washer. This method allows straps to be aligned to sit in tile valleys whilst providing a secure fixing between the roof and the solar collectors. Other collector types have different methods to achieve sturdy fastening from the collector to the structural roof timber.

method 2: threaded rods on a pitched roof

In the case of a slate roof where all slates are nailed it can be impractical to use alloy straps as per method 1. Threaded rods and right-angled brackets can be used instead to fix the collectors.

Right-angled brackets can be manufactured from short pieces of aluminium strap or a full-length, aluminium, right-angled rail. The slight advantage to using full length rails is that collectors can be bolted together (via the rails), ensuring pipe connections are accurately aligned.

On a 2 collector system, each collector will have four threaded rods attached, fairly evenly spaced but *avoiding* rafters when penetrating the roof.

locating rafters beneath fastened roof coverings

To locate rafters on a roof where the main weatherproof covering is completely nailed down (such as a slate roof with secondary roofing felt), slide a length of thin flexible metal strapping (or builder's fixing band) between the felt overlap from inside the roof space.

With a little encouragement the other end of the strapping will slide between the rows of slate and appear on the outside of the roof. Move the strapping from side to side until it meets the edge of a rafter. The rafter's edge can then be marked on the slates or fixed tiles above.

Decide where (from left to right of the collectors) you will drill holes through the roof covering, ideally aiming for holes in the peak of tiles (if they are not slates or flat tiles) and taking care to *avoid any* rafters beneath.

Fit the brackets in line with these positions to a temporary straight length of sturdy timber (the timber is only required if you are *not* using full-length right-angled rails).

Drill holes in each of the right-angled brackets and through the roof covering, taking care to drill perpendicular to the roof tiles. Use the drilled brackets attached to sturdy timber (or full-length rail) as a template to drill holes in a suitable timber plank to be used as the fixing batten in the loft space; this could be similar in dimensions to the collector batten described in method 1, page 175.

Cut four threaded rods to roughly the length required (for example, 500mm should suffice for non-flat profiled tiles), attach them loosely to the right-angle brackets and pass the end of the rods through the roof tile holes.

In the loft space place nuts, washers and the predrilled timber plank onto the threaded rod ends as shown in fig 114 and fix the plank to the underside of the rafters using coach screws.

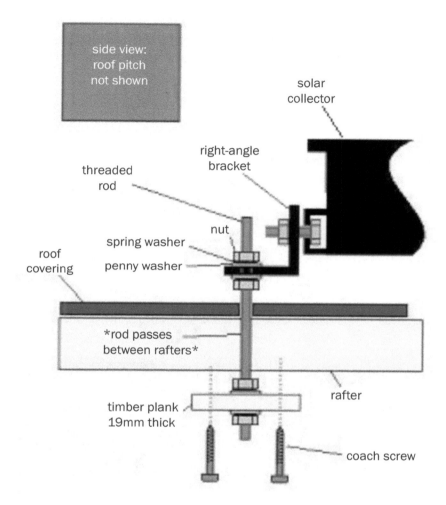

side view: roof pitch not shown

solar collector

right-angle bracket

threaded rod

nut

spring washer

roof covering

penny washer

rod passes between rafters

rafter

timber plank 19mm thick

coach screw

NOTE: Seal all holes in roof coverings with high performance silicone sealant

fig 114: threaded rod method

The exact position of the external right-angled brackets or full length rail can now be adjusted and fixed by nuts and washers.

The collectors can be bolted to the bottom right-angled brackets and pieces of wood placed beneath to temporarily space the top edge of the collectors away from the roof tiles whilst the top right-angled brackets are positioned.

The top right-angle brackets can now be temporarily bolted to the top of the collectors. Once the hole positions are marked onto the roof tiles beneath, the top brackets can be removed and holes drilled through the roof covering to accept the threaded rods.

A similar process can now be used for mounting the top right-angled brackets or full length rail.

Once the collectors are secured, the remaining threaded rod can be trimmed and the temporary wooden spacers removed from beneath the collectors.

fig 115: fixing batten in the loft space

method 3: large coach screws on a pitched roof

A variation on method 2 with a similar process but using large coach screws instead of threaded rods.

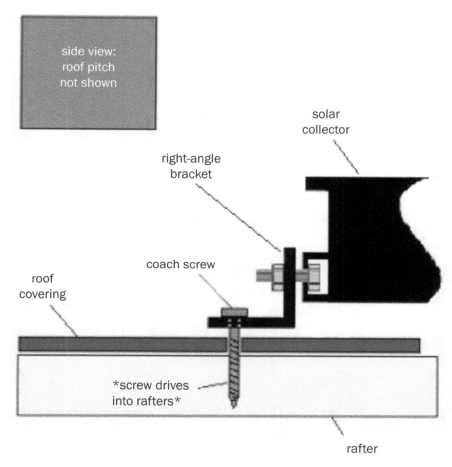

side view:
roof pitch
not shown

solar
collector

right-angle
bracket

coach screw

roof
covering

*screw drives
into rafters*

rafter

NOTE: Seal all holes in roof coverings with
high performance silicone sealant

fig 116: coach screw method

Holes are drilled into the roof covering to allow the coach screws to fix directly to rafters beneath.

The coach screws used should be weather resistant, of a sufficient length and should be fixed into rafters of a sound condition to a depth which ensures safe load bearing of the solar collectors on the roof (for example, a screw fixed only 25mm into a timber rafter is *not* sufficient to secure the weight of solar collectors; a minimum of 70mm is recommended).

method 4: flat roof mounting frames

Flat roof mounting can provide a wide range of challenges. If you intend to mount your solar collectors on a flat roof or the ground, the components required will differ from a pitched roof mounting kit and will include aluminium, stainless steel or galvanised steel bars and angle brackets to make a mounting frame (depending on the collector model).

The frame consists of 2 or 3 triangular frames (for a 2 or 3 Atlas collector system respectively) joined together by cross braces at the rear and the collector rails at the front.

fig 117: bolting together the sections of the frame

fig 118: triangular frame

The length of steel shown in the circle in fig 118 will need to be cut off and the exposed end protected against corrosion with suitable paint-on inhibitor as shown in fig 120.

fig 119: the triangular frames should be cross braced at the back

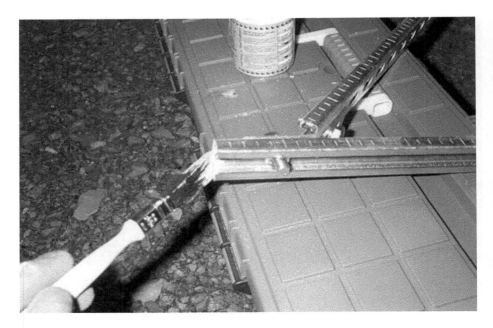

fig 120: protect exposed ends against corrosion

fig 121: completed triangular frames

Flat roof mounting frames can be fixed to the roof in a variety of ways and each flat roof will be different. After careful consideration of relevant issues (such as the strength of the roof structure, whether to drill holes through the flat roof, the material composition of the roof itself and it's covering) you may decide to fix the collectors to the roof using one of the following methods:

- fit weather resistant timber bearers onto the roof (bolted underneath to structural timber), dress with bitumen and felt and screw the collector mounting frame onto the bearers (see fig 122).
- sit the collector mounting frame on UV-resistant, hollow rubber feet and pass a bolt from the frame through the feet, through the roof and onto structural timber underneath. Weather seal with high performance silicone sealant. This method is not considered to be durable and is only suitable in limited situations.

fig 122: roof collector mounted on weather-resistant timber bearers

If drilling holes into the flat roof is out of the question, you may want to try:

- constructing a frame spanning the width of the roof and securing it to the side walls of the building. The collector mounting frame can be fixed to this.

- use ballast to hold the collector frame to the roof. Paving slabs or concrete blocks are both heavy ballast that can be drilled to accept masonry fixings.
- heavy ballast can also be adhered to the roof using silicone sealant. As the structure is not mechanically fixed to the roof this technique requires a careful assessment of the site to ensure the ballast is capable of securing collectors during the strongest foreseeable wind conditions. If this method is chosen it is also important to seal around the entire edge of each ballast block or slab. This will prevent water from penetrating between the blocks or slabs and the roof covering which, in winter months, could expand when freezing and break the bonding seal.

Whatever the chosen method, it is important to consider the load-bearing capacity of the roof, health and safety and local planning conditions. If in doubt seek the advice of a roofing professional, planning advisor or structural engineer.

collector to collector connections

BOA fittings for use with Atlas collectors
The heating fluid travels from one Atlas collector to the next via a stainless steel flexible connector (BOA fitting) comprising:
- 2 x clamps with screws
- 2 x rubber 'o' rings
- 1 x flexible mini tube

It is important to ensure the mating surfaces of the BOA fitting and the collector pipe fitting are aligned and that the 'o' ring is in place (there is a slight recess in the mating surface of the collector pipe fitting for this).

fig 123: a BOA fitting clamped to one collector

collector sensor (RESOL)

The collector's sensor is identified by a *black* cable (do not use a different sensor unless colour coding dictates in the manufacturer's instructions).

sensors for Atlas collectors

The sensor for the collectors should be placed in the sensor pocket (make sure you push it right inside) on the top right hand side of the last collector (closest to the flow pipe). This should be weather sealed and secured using a small amount of silicone sealant .

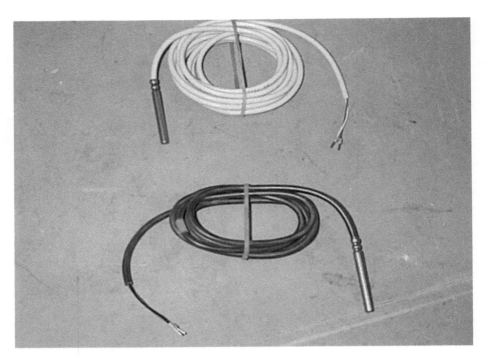

fig 124: collector sensor

fig 125: Atlas collector sensor connection

There is a second sensor pocket on the bottom left side of the first collector which is unused. This should also be sealed.

sensors for Type 3000 collectors

The sensor for the collectors should be placed in the sensor pocket forming part of the Sensor Tee assembly (make sure you push it right inside) on the 'hot' outlet (flow) pipe at the top of the last collector.

The cable for the sensor should be taken through the roof to the loftspace and any hole made should be weather sealed

For the wiring of the collector sensor, please refer to the RESOL controller manual.

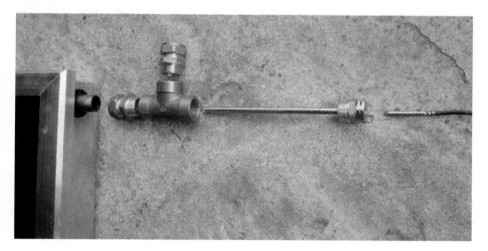

fig 126: disassembled sensor tee

pipe connections

Hot and cold pipe outlets (flow and return respectively) from the collector array are 22mm copper pipes for both the Atlas and Type 3000 collectors. A compression reducing coupler should be fitted to each pipe outlet and a suitable length of bent 15mm copper pipe inserted. The 15mm copper pipe should be bent as required to pass through holes drilled in the roof covering.

After tightening the compression fittings, Armaflex HT insulation should be placed around the pipes and fittings and secured with weather-resistant black tape (Armaflex also manufacture tape for this purpose).

fig 127: completed, insulated pipe connection

weather sealing

All holes through the roof should be thoroughly cleaned and generously weather sealed using suitable silicone sealant.

The process of cleaning surfaces and applying silicone sealant is critical to its performance and it is important to make sure surfaces are clean and dry for good adhesion. The pictorial guide in fig 128 should help.

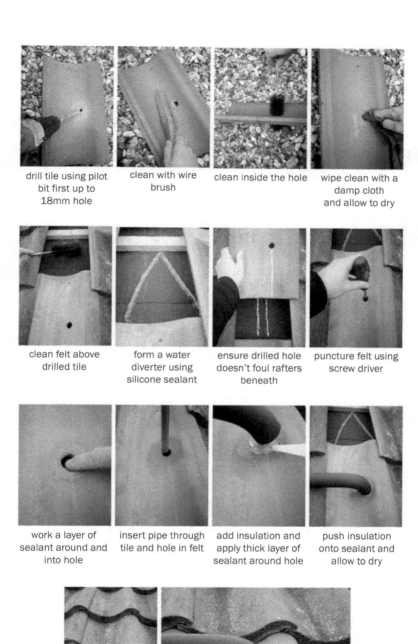

drill tile using pilot bit first up to 18mm hole

clean with wire brush

clean inside the hole

wipe clean with a damp cloth and allow to dry

clean felt above drilled tile

form a water diverter using silicone sealant

ensure drilled hole doesn't foul rafters beneath

puncture felt using screw driver

work a layer of sealant around and into hole

insert pipe through tile and hole in felt

add insulation and apply thick layer of sealant around hole

push insulation onto sealant and allow to dry

refit surrounding roof tiles

the finished article

fig 128: weather sealing process

alternative weather sealing methods

lead soaker

A lead soaker is essentially a square of lead with an upstand fabricated with a sufficient internal diameter to allow solar fluid pipes to pass through the roof.

lead soaker with a copper upstand

lead soaker with a silicone rubber upstand

fig 129: lead soaker

A hole is drilled in the chosen roof tile and the lead soaker placed over the drilled hole and moulded to closely match the shape of the tile profile beneath. The pipe is passed through and any remaining gap is filled using silicone sealant.

custom-made roof tile

A roof tile exactly matching those on the roof is manufactured with a 'hood' to allow solar fluid pipes to pass through. Gaps around pipes can be filled with off-cuts of pipe insulation.

special hooded tile for passing solar pipes through roof covering

(shown here with special solar pipes)

fig 130: custom-made roof tile

This solution can look very nice when completed but each tile usually needs to be specially manufactured by a roofing supplies specialist, which requires waiting time and extra expense.

notes and tips:

- **if you are fixing collectors to the roof on a sunny day,** take great care when touching any pipework from the collectors and once fitted, try to cover the collectors as soon as possible. This will reduce the risk of burning yourself on hot pipes.
- **You should try to avoid using a drill on hammer action** when drilling roof tiles as many tile materials will shatter when drilled using hammer action.
- **consider removing or 'sliding up' a selection of roof tiles** to make foot holes for moving around; be sure to check first that the roof area is of suitable strength and condition (for example, no rotten tile battens or cracked rafters).
- **it isn't a good idea to use any roof-fixed collector mountings** as a temporary footings as this may deform the fixings, causing problems when attaching the collectors.

- **when tightening or loosening stainless steel nuts and bolts**, a very small amount of lubricant (for example, grease) will help prevent the nut / bolt from seizing up whilst turning.
- **to get uniform bends in all of your mounting straps,** try bending each strap around the same 'former' such as a piece of 4" x 2" wood. The actual size of the 'former' will depend upon the gap (if any) you want to create between the valley of your tiles and the underside of your collectors.

installing other components

the hot water cylinder

All of the hot water cylinders (HWC) shown here are 'open vented' (supplied with water under gravity from a cold water storage cistern above the level of the cylinder) and indirect (the water circulating in the solar collectors is separate from the water delivered to your taps). There are four main cylinder variants shown here, but many other variants are commercially available.

HWC size #1:
1350mm x 400mm 150 litres
twin coil grade 3
50mm insulation
primary coil to heat 100 litres

HWC size #2:
1500mm x 450mm 215 litres
twin coil grade 3
50mm insulation
primary coil to heat 120 litres

HWC size #3:
1800mm x 450mm 260 litres
twin coil grade 3
50mm insulation
primary coil to heat 150 litres

HWC size #4:
1250mm x 400mm 138 litres
single coil grade 3
50mm insulation

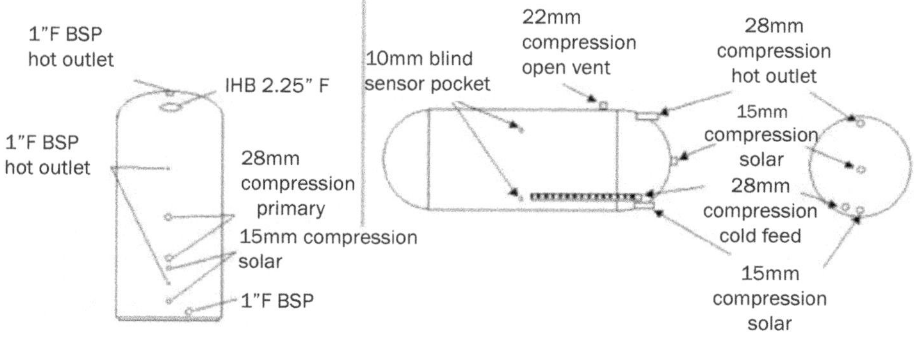

fig 131: the four main cylinder variants

The cylinders illustrated in fig 131 are as follows: the vertical cylinder shown on the left is of the twin coil type. This type of cylinder is designed to replace your existing cylinder and be connected to your existing boiler and hot water distribution pipework.

The solar coil is at the bottom of the cylinder and can therefore heat all of the water above it (assuming there is sufficient solar energy).

Above the solar coil is the boiler coil, which is capable of heating around 100 litres of water (120 and 150 for medium and large cylinders respectively) each time the boiler is switched on. There is also a fitting in the dome of the cylinder for an immersion heater if required.

The horizontal cylinder shown on the right is smaller, and of the single-solar-coil, preheating type. This type of cylinder is designed for installation in your loft space, interrupting the cold feed pipework between your cold water storage cistern and your existing hot water cylinder (which remains installed).

The solar coil heats all of the water in this preheat cylinder (assuming there is sufficient solar energy) and then passes this water to your existing hot water cylinder for onward delivery to your household taps etc.

The solar preheated water in this cylinder takes longer to reach outlets (taps, showers) and this time delay increases the potential heat loss from the overall system. However, the preheat cylinder cannot be heated by any other means, which can improve solar energy yield as there is no chance the backup water heater can accidentally displace solar energy. The building regulations for England and Wales now require a backup heat source in this type of cylinder, in order to ensure the stored water occasionally reaches a high enough temperature to kill bacteria – something that cannot be guaranteed using solar energy alone.

The cylinder dimensions shown are approximate and do not include the encasing 50mm insulation.

The tappings are as follows:
- 1" BSP female hot outlet; to accept 1" male fitting adaptor for copper pipe, connecting to your existing hot distribution pipework, to taps, etc.
- IHB 2.25"; this fits a standard electric immersion heater or can be capped off if not required.
- 10mm blind sensor pockets; to allow convenient fitting of the solar temperature sensors. An upper sensor pocket is included in the event that you choose to upgrade solar controller and use more sensors.
- 28mm compression primary; to accept copper pipe, connecting to your existing boiler pipework.

- 28mm compression cold feed; to accept copper pipe, connecting to the pipe supplying cold water to your existing or previous hot water cylinder.
- 15mm compression solar; connecting to the solar pipework.

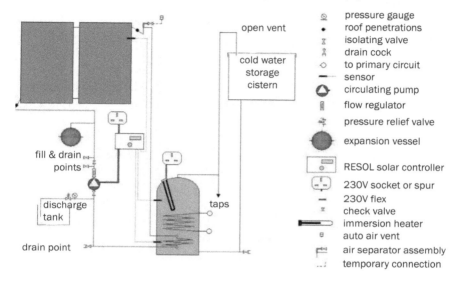

fig 132: an open vented, vertical solar hot water cylinder in a typical sealed and pressurised solar installation (with advanced solar controller shown)

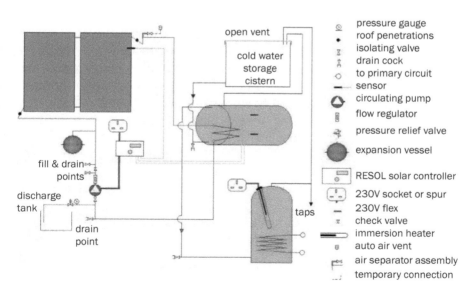

fig 133: an open vented, horizontal solar hot water cylinder in a typical sealed and pressurised solar installation (with advanced solar controller shown)

installing the cylinder

Installing the cylinder is perhaps the most difficult part of fitting the solar water heating system and I recommend you take the time to understand your existing pipe layout *before* removing anything and, if it helps, label pipes and valves.

note on compliance

The installation of a solar hot water cylinder to a UK dwelling should now be notified under the building regulations to the local authority Building Inspector, to ensure work complies with the regulations. There are excellent guides available explaining all aspects of the building regulations (which change from time to time). If you are concerned about how to comply, you should consult a guide book, speak to your Building Inspector or contract an approved competent plumber to undertake this part of the installation.

The following steps are an example of how to change a conventional open vented, indirect cylinder to an open vented solar *twin coil* cylinder (the more complex of the two types illustrated).

- ensure you have plenty of working space; remove airing shelves etc.
- switch off the boiler and isolate power to any immersion heater
- have some rags handy in case of spillages
- isolate the water supply entering the cold feed pipe to the cylinder (either by closing a gate valve on the cold feed pipe or tying the cold water storage cistern's ball valve up to a piece of overhanging wood or pipe)
- isolate the liquid entering the primary (boiler circuit) pipes (either by closing a gate valve on the feed pipe or tying the cold water storage tank's ball valve up to a piece of overhanging wood or pipe)
- in the case of a sealed and pressurised primary circuit, open the discharge valve to expel pressure
- drain the *primary* pipework via a convenient drain cock (for example underneath a radiator or next to the boiler) using a hose pipe. This will require the introduction of air at a high point in the circuit (perhaps by opening an air vent)
- drain the cylinder's hot water (the *secondary* water) using a hose pipe (there is usually a drain cock connected to the cold feed pipe or directly off the cylinder)
- open the hot taps on the bath and the basin
- remove the cylinder thermostat from the side of the cylinder
- disconnect the immersion heater, noting the colour coding of wires

fig 134: drain cock

- once the cylinder has emptied, check that the ball valves on the cold water storage tank (the large one) and the boiler header tank (the small tank) are not dripping or running (if it is and you are isolating via a gate valve, the valve is not completely closed; you will need to drain the cistern).
- with the cylinder empty, cut into the hot distribution pipe just above the cylinder and the cold feed pipe somewhere below the gate valve
- cut into the two primary pipes at a convenient location
- remove any hose pipes and clear the exit route for the cylinder
- when moving the old cylinder, be careful not to spill any small amount of fluid held inside; firmly plugging the holes with rags can help. Rock the old cylinder from side to side before attempting to move, to check that most of the water has been drained out.

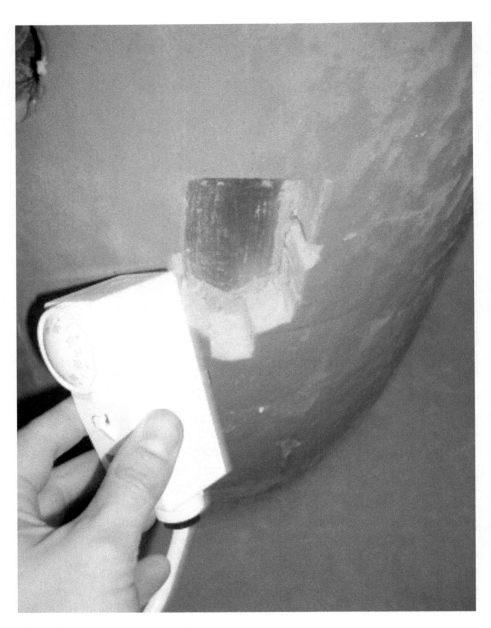

fig 135: removing cylinder thermostat

fig 136: disconnect the immersion heater

fig 137: the empty cylinder, ready to be moved

preparing for the new vertical solar cylinder

It may be necessary or just more convenient (in terms of working space) to modify some of the pipework before the new cylinder goes in; things to consider are:

- the location of any thermostatic mixing valves in proximity to the cylinder (if you have chosen this option)
- primary pipe (those connecting to the boiler) alterations
- cold feed pipe route (from the cold water storage cistern)
- if any of the gate valves are faulty, replace them now
- if the primary or secondary vent pipes are 15mm diameter, they should be replaced with at least 22mm pipes
- extending the immersion heater flex (if required)
- moving the immersion heater spur box
- fitting a new cylinder plinth (air circulation beneath the cylinder can prevent condensation and rotting of floorboards)
- repairing or replacing any sections of damaged floor

fitting the new vertical solar cylinder

- look inside the new cylinder; check that nothing has fallen inside
- fit the immersion heater into the cylinder (if refitting old immersion, use a new fibre gasket)
- fit any adaptors to tappings on the new cylinder
- once everything is prepared, move the cylinder into position and rotate it so that all tappings are reasonably accessible
- connect up primary and secondary pipes as required, ensuring any motorised valves and air release devices previously on primary pipes are returned. To avoid unnecessary heat loss, the secondary hot outlet pipe from the top of the cylinder should ideally travel horizontally for 450mm/18" before any vertical pipes are connected (the open vent pipe should always be the first).

fig 138: outlet pipe from top of cylinder

- with all pipework amended (double check all joints are soldered or tightened), refill secondary pipework from cold water storage cistern and check for leaks.
- if there are no leaks, refill primary pipework from boiler header tank (or charge from feed pipe if it is a sealed or pressurised system) and check for leaks. It's a good idea at this point to add a corrosion inhibitor to this tank before too much water is added.
- if there are no leaks, turn on the hot taps to check flow and remove trapped air. Leave running to allow new pipes and cylinder internal walls to be flushed.
- cut a new hole in the cylinder insulation and refit the cylinder thermostat (this should be between the two *primary* tappings; use the old cylinder as a guide for exact positioning between these tappings).
- vent trapped air, switch on the boiler for heating and hot water and remove further trapped air via air screws and radiator air caps. Check that all the radiators and cylinder reach the required temperature.
- rewire the immersion heater and check that it works
- insulate all necessary pipes

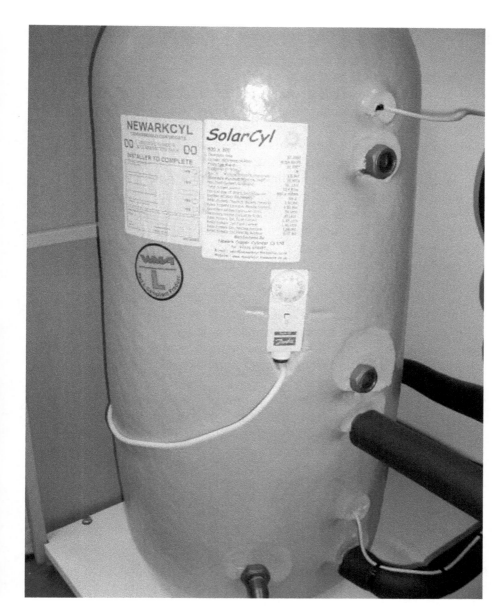

fig 139: cylinder thermostat

The following steps are an example of how to fit an open vented, solar, *single coil* cylinder, which is easier to install than the twin coil type already described.

preparing for and fitting the new horizontal solar cylinder

- decide where the new solar cylinder will be (try to keep pipe runs to a minimum to reduce heat loss)
- fit the new cylinder cradles (use sturdy timber cut to suit, such as 4"x2") to spread the weight and prevent the cylinder from rolling sideways. The location should be able to easily carry the weight of the cylinder (as stated by the manufacturer) plus the weight of the water inside (approx 1 litre = 1kg) plus the weight of the installer!
- look inside the new cylinder; check that nothing has fallen inside
- once everything is prepared, move the cylinder into position and rotate it so that all tappings are reasonably accessible (try to have at least 150mm vertical distance between the bottom of the cold water storage cistern and the top of the solar cylinder)
- isolate the cold water supply pipe (rising main) to the cold water storage cistern in your loft
- open hot water taps to drain the cold water storage cistern
- cut into the cold feed pipe (secondary pipework) from the cold water storage cistern to the existing hot water cylinder
- run new pipework (at least the same diameter as the existing pipe) from the cistern to the cold feed tapping of your new solar cylinder (use as few tight radius bends as possible)
- run new pipework from the hot outlet of your solar cylinder to your existing cylinder (as described in the vertical cylinder fitting above, the first section of pipe should be horizontal); also run a new vent pipe from your solar cylinder terminating above the existing cold water storage cistern
- with all pipework amended (double check all joints are soldered or tightened), refill the cold water storage cistern and secondary pipework and check for leaks
- insulate all necessary pipes

Naturally, hot water systems in homes are the subject of a host of adaptations throughout their working life, and as a result may require a different sequence of tasks to undertake the installation of a new solar hot water cylinder than those detailed above.

It is worth mentioning that a solar preheat hot water cylinder doesn't have to be horizontal; the concept works for vertical preheat cylinders too (though it can often be more difficult to find a suitable location for a vertical solar preheat cylinder and horizontal cylinders can usually be installed in the loft space below the level of the cold water storage tank).

pump and safety set

This design features a hand-made pump and safety set which can be constructed from individual components by most people with only very basic DIY experience. Factory-assembled pump and safety sets are also available but are not covered here.

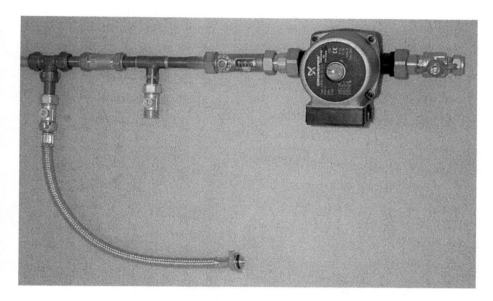

fig 140: hand-made pump and safety net

The hand-made pump and safety set can be fitted: '
- horizontally in the loft space, screwed to joists
- horizontally in the loft space, screwed to the underside of pitched roof rafters
- vertically in the loft space: screwed between a joist and a rafter
- vertically in your airing cupboard (recommended)

The pump can be fitted vertically or horizontally provided that its motor shaft axis is horizontal and the pump's electrical connections are not positioned below the motor shaft axis (the installation manual supplied with a circulating pump provides further details).

The pump set should be secured with suitable screws and fixings as required.

Your choice of location will depend upon:
• space for components in your airing cupboard or storage vessel location
• space in which to work
• cables you will need to extend; the further away from your (DTC) controller, the longer the power cable needed for the pump
• pipe routes around existing obstacles
• suitable wall timber or roof joists on which to mount your pump set
• remember to try and keep the pipes from your solar collectors to the solar hot water cylinder as short as possible; longer pipes slightly increase cost and reduce efficiency

fig 141: circulating pump

The components of the pump set and their respective functions are:

the pump (circulation of fluid) and pump valves

Isolating the pump for the purposes of replacement; to the right of the pump is a butterfly valve. There is another valve built into the flow regulator to the left of the pump. As you can see in fig 141 the screw head on the face of the pump can be used to expel air and provide access to a further screw head behind, which is used to check if the motor shaft has seized.

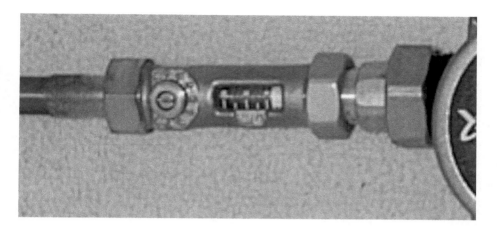

fig 142: *the flow regulator (visual confirmation and fine tuning of fluid flow rate)*

the non-return valve (NRV)

The NRV is positioned between the tee connections, see fig 143, to prevent gravity heat loss from the hot water cylinder to the solar collectors at night. There is a direction of flow arrow on the NRV casing. The NRV should be high temperature rated.

There are valves leading from each of the tee connections. When filling the system, fluid enters the system through the valve on the left (commissioning valve A) and travels around the system until it reaches the valve on the right (commissioning valve B). These valves are used to expel most of the air in the system before the pump is activated.

When draining the system via the drain cock at the lowest point (on the cold pipe assembly, attached to the solar heat exchange coil on your hot water cylinder), the two valves can be connected together using a braided flexible hose. Both valves are then opened and fluid above the NRV is able to drain down.

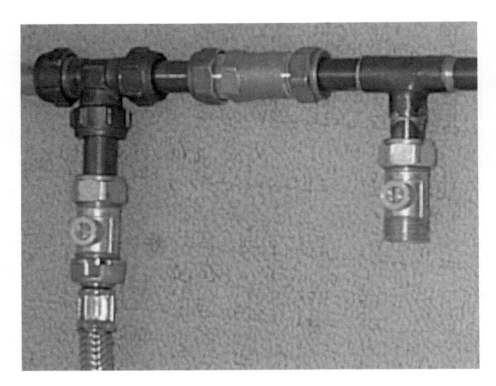

fig 143: non-return valve

In the event of a fault within the system, excess fluid pressure is discharged from the pressure relief valve into a suitable container.

Note: the discharge container should be capable of retaining fluid at near boiling point without distorting and should be positioned on a stable base, not sitting directly on loft insulation or a ceiling board.

fig 144: the pressure relief valve and pressure gauge to monitor and regulate pressure in the system

expansion set

The expansion vessel consists of a metal casing with a fluid entry point on one end (the fluid side) and a gas adjustment valve on the opposite end (the gas pre-charge side). The term 'gas' is used here to describe nitrogen or air, and not flammable or explosive gas mixtures.

The expansion set is designed to allow expansion and contraction of the system's fluid content whilst maintaining a working pressure.

fig 145: expansion vessel

The gas pre-charge pressure can be altered using a bicycle or foot pump and air pressure gauge attached to the vessel's gas adjustment valve.

fig 146: gas adjustment valve

To help protect components from potential damage caused by high temperature fluid, the branch pipe leading to the expansion vessel should be installed at least one metre from the NRV (in the pump and safety set), and where there is less than 3 linear metres of pipe between the expansion vessel and the nearest collector, the branch pipe should be at least 3 metres long.

electrics and wiring

Do not attempt to modify any electrical components without first isolating the supply.

If you are in any doubt, seek advice before working on 220-240 volt electrical supply, or employ a competent person.

The solar hot water system detailed here is designed to be wired into a fused connection unit (spur) or British Standard 3-pin plug. You may already have a spare spur or plug socket close to the intended location of your solar controller (all solar equipment is powered via the controller). If this is not the case, it is a good idea to employ a competent person to fit the new spur or socket you will need.

The only other wiring you may need to do when installing is:
- extending 230 volt supply cable from spur or socket to the solar controller
- extending 230 volt supply cable from the controller to the pump
- extending sensor 1 cable (the black sheathed sensor cable) to the collector on the roof
- extending sensor 2 cable to the new solar hot water cylinder
- fitting or replacing Earth bonding cables between pipes around your solar hot water cylinder

sensors

Sensor cables are extra low voltage and not 'polarity sensitive' making wiring to an extension cable simple (see below). The black-sheathed sensor cable is UV and high-temperature resistant and the light grey sheathed sensor cable is only designed for use in the sensor pockets of the hot water cylinder.

Note: Other brands may feature a different colour coding.

When wiring sensors, ensure wires are connected to correct terminals in the controller; your system will not work properly if wired incorrectly.

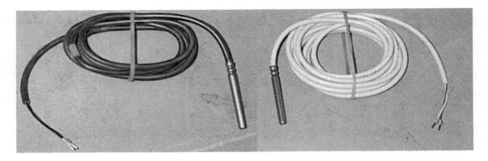

fig 147: sensor cables

There are 2 different cables that should be run alongside the fluid-carrying pipes:
- a 2 core flex with a minimum cross-sectional area of 0.5mm^2 is used to extend sensor 1 (black sheathed) from the solar collector to the controller via a suitable junction box, see fig 148
- a 3 core flex with a minimum cross-sectional area of 0.75mm^2 is required to connect the 230 volt supply for the pump, and the main electricity supply to the solar controller

When running cables near solar fluid pipes, you should ensure that
- cables are adequately fixed along their full length
- cables cannot touch any pipe surface as even the 'cold' (return) pipe can exceed 80°C
- The sensor and sensor extension cables (2 core) are not run directly alongside higher voltage cables, as these cables may create interference to the sensor signal. A minimum spacing of 50mm is suggested when running sensor and power cables in parallel.
- cables are extended using a cable type that is suitable for the task: it should have sufficient current-carrying capacity and, if the cable will not be carrying 220-240 volt AC then it must be visibly dissimilar or clearly marked so as to distinguish it from household power cables

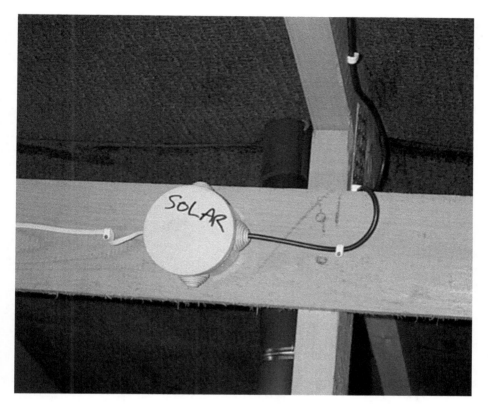

fig 148: clearly marked junction box

wiring the pump in

There is a plastic wiring box on the side of the pump. Inside this box are three terminal connections, each clearly marked as follows:

L - the brown sheathed wire in the 3 core cable is connected here.

N - the blue sheathed wire in the 3 core cable is connected here.

E - the yellow and green sheathed wire in the 3 core cable is connected here. The following symbol is sometimes used instead of 'E':

Before terminating any wires from the 3 core cable in the pump, ensure you first pass the 3 core cable through the pump's cable gland; this is the point where the cable should enter the plastic wiring box and includes a tightening nut.

The nut should tighten onto the outer white sheathing of the cable, preventing strain on individual coloured wires in the event of the cable being pulled.

Further information on wiring the pump will be available from the manufacturer's instruction booklet.

fig 149: pump wiring

pump speeds

The pump features a three speed selector on the outside of the plastic wiring box. Speed selection is covered in the *commissioning and troubleshooting* section, see page 225.

wiring the controller

The following information relates to a RESOL 'AX' type solar controller.

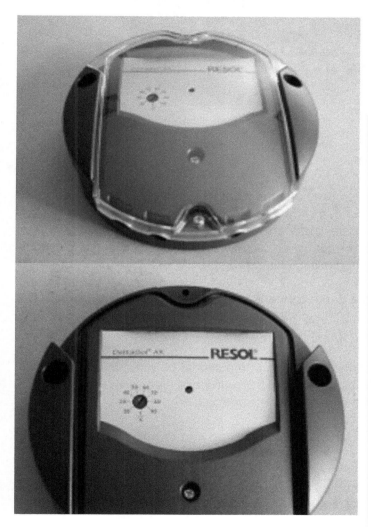

fig 150: access to the controller connections

The terminal connections for all cables can be accessed by removing the outer clear plastic and inner black plastic covers.

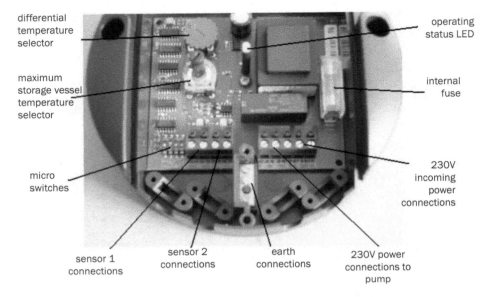

differential temperature selector

maximum storage vessel temperature selector

micro switches

operating status LED

internal fuse

230V incoming power connections

sensor 1 connections

sensor 2 connections

earth connections

230V power connections to pump

fig 151: the covers removed and main components identified

Power and sensor cables enter and leave the controller via cable retainers along the bottom of the controller, see fig 151. The inner cover has tabs that can be snapped off to pass cables through.

Incoming power (the cable connected to a plug or fused spur) should be wired into terminals 10 (blue wire) and 11 (brown wire) with the yellow and green wire terminating at any spare point on the earth connection block.

The power cable connected to the pump should be wired into terminals 7 (brown wire) and 9 (blue wire) with the yellow and green wire terminating at any spare point on the earth connection block.

Sensor 1 extension cable should be wired into terminals 1 and 2 (in no particular order).

Sensor 2 cable (from the storage vessel) should be wired into terminals 3 and 4 (in no particular order).

controller features explained

operating status LED: this shows a stable or flashing colour which denotes the operating status of the controller.

internal fuse (4 Amp): protects the controller from overvoltage. It's a good idea to place a standard 3 Amp fuse in the plug or spur supplying power to the controller.

differential temperature selector: This sets the value at which the controller activates the pump. It is factory-set to around 5 or 6 K, which is perfect for most installations.

maximum storage vessel temperature selector (Tmax): This is the maximum temperature the solar thermal system is allowed to heat the storage vessel before deactivating the pump. Factory-set to around 60°C (recommended).

micro switches: There are four micro switches, each performing a different function.

switch 1: manual operation. In the 'off' position, the controller works automatically by comparing temperatures in the collector and storage vessel. Switch to 'on' if you need to activate the pump (only needed during commissioning).

switch 2: maximum temperature limitation. This should always be 'on' for this system design.

switch 3: antifreeze protection. This is an electronic frost protection function and is not used in this system design, therefore it should always be 'off'.

switch 4: minimum temperature limitation. This is not used in this system design so should always be 'off'.

Further information for this type of controller will be covered in the installation documents provided by the manufacturer.

supplementary earth bonding

Supplementary earth bonding consists of thick green- and yellow-sheathed wires with special clamps which are designed to provide a low resistance safety circuit in the event of an electrical fault somewhere in the house.

If you are installing new metal components (for example, a new hot water cylinder), there may be a need to fit supplementary bonding to all metal surfaces that are considered an electrocution risk (if in doubt, consult a qualified electrician) and if you had existing bonding cables around the hot water cylinder, then these should be reattached.

fig 152: earth bonding

If you need further guidance on supplementary earth bonding, seek advice from a trained electrical installer.

commissioning and troubleshooting

This is the stage at which the system components are installed and ready for inspection, testing and setting to work.

The first thing you may need to do is to mix up heat transfer fluid (further details below; this only applies if you have purchased a concentrated antifreeze such as Tyfocor L which is colourless). Surplus heat transfer fluid can be stored in a sealed container for future top-up (if ever required) and we recommend the container is clearly labelled.

The following describes the commissioning procedure for a system containing a hand-made pump and safety set and a RESOL AX solar controller, see page 221, installed where the vertical distance between the solar collectors and the expansion vessel is no more than 5 metres.

Other system components and configurations may require a different sequence of events.

Note: the first complete fill is water only – no antifreeze.
- check that valves adjoining either side of pump are open, the flow regulator is set to maximum flow (screw head in line with the body of the flow regulator), and any arrows stamped on the pump, valves, etc. are in the correct direction of flow
- double-check that sensors are secured in the correct positions and (with the power disconnected) that all wiring is correct
- verify, using a tyre pressure gauge, that the gas precharge of the expansion vessel is set to 0.8 bar (and afterwards, check that the air adjustment valve is not leaking using a small amount of soapy water applied to the end of the valve)
- ensure any manual air-bleed screws and drain cocks in solar pipes are closed
- cover solar collectors to prevent them heating up
- ensure the air-separation assembly, shown in fig 153, is installed correctly. Connect the temporary automatic air vent to the air-separation assembly, open the isolation valve (which must be high-temperature tolerant) and unscrew the cap of the automatic air vent.

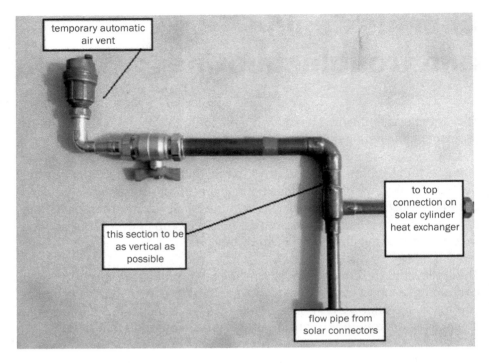

temporary automatic
air vent

this section to be
as vertical as
possible

to top
connection on
solar cylinder
heat exchanger

flow pipe from
solar connectors

fig 153: air separation assembly

- double-check all pipe connections have been tightened or soldered
- to fill the system; first fill the hand-filling bottle with fluid (the first complete fill is *water only*) and pump up the pressure in the bottle
- connect the bottle hose to 'commissioning valve A' near the non-return valve (see *pump and safety set* section, page 209, for details)
- place a bucket or container under 'commissioning valve B' and open the valve
- open valve on bottle to release fluid into system
- top up the reservoir and pump up the filling bottle as required
- you will see water through the glass on the flow regulator, and the pressure gauge may start to register pressure. Close 'commissioning valve B' and the pressure will increase. At around 0.8 to 1 bar, the pressure rise will slow as the expansion vessel starts to accept fluid. Close 'commissioning valve A' and check all components for leaks.
- if any leaks are discovered, join together 'commissioning valves 'A' and 'B' using the flexible hose from the hand-filling bottle and open both valves. Drain fluid from the lowest drain point in solar pipes, repair leaks, reset valve positions and repeat the filling process to this stage.

Note: once fluid has started draining you will need to open the isolating valve in the air separation assembly and blow down the pipe end to *fully* drain the system.

- if there are no leaks, add more fluid from the hand-filling bottle through 'commissioning valve A' until the pressure reads at least 2.5 bar up to as much as 3 bar. Close 'commissioning valve A'.
- place a rag or container under the pump face and loosen the air screw. A hissing sound denotes air leaving the pump. The screw can be tightened when the hissing stops.
- the system should be switched on to allow the pump to dislodge trapped air. This is done by moving micro switch one setting to the 'on' position (using a RESOL AX controller) and switching the power supply on. Pressure may drop as air is expelled from the automatic air vent attached to the air-separation assembly. Pressure should then stabilise.
- to help remove any air bubbles, try varying the speed of the pump via the pump's speed selector.
- check for leaks, drain and repair if necessary. Once repaired, repeat the process to this stage.
- the flow regulator will initially register an irregular flow rate, followed by a stable flow rate which indicates the majority of the air has been expelled, pipes are connected together correctly and there are no blockages. If no flow rate registers, this may be caused by air or other blockages, closed valves, non-return valve is installed backwards or pipes are installed incorrectly.
- return the pump to speed number 1 and let it run for 20 minutes.
- assuming pressure and flow are stable, switch the pump off, connect together commissioning valves 'A' and 'B' using flexible hose from the hand-filling bottle, place a container beneath the drain point and drain down fluid from the system.
  Note: once fluid has started draining you will need to detach the temporary automatic air vent, open the isolating valve in the air-separation assembly and blow down the pipe end to *fully* drain the system.
- drained fluid should be discarded.
- refill the system and pressurise as previously described, this time with pre-mixed heat transfer fluid until pressure reaches around 1.5 to 2 bar (see chart for mix ratio if using Tyfocor L concentrated antifreeze).

Tyfocor L (vol. %)	Frost protection (deg. C)
25	-10.7
30	-14
35	-17.6
40	-21.5
45	-26
50	-32.4
55	-40.4

fig 154: Tyfocor mix ratios

If using premixed antifreeze, do not dilute it with water (use as supplied)

- switch on the pump as previously described to remove air from the system
- once air is removed (so that the flow regulator registers a stable flow and the pump is reasonably quiet in operation), close the isolating valve attached to the air-separation assembly and remove the temporary automatic air vent
- set the fluid flow to the recommended rate (approximately 1 to 1.5 litres per minute *per collector*; measured from the lower edge of the indicator in the sight glass) by selecting a pump speed that achieves the minimum recommended flow and then trimming the rate by partially closing the adjuster on the flow regulator
- isolate the power to the system (at plug or fused spur) and reset the controller micro switch one setting to 'off'. This will allow controller to operate the system for information supplied by the temperature sensors.
- place a discharge container under the discharge pipe and test the operation of the pressure relief valve (by quickly turning the plastic top through 90°). Fluid should pass into the discharge container and the valve should re-close, stopping further flow. Repeat this until the static-fluid pressure (when the pump is not running) for the system registers 1.5 bar.
- make a final check for leaks and fit any remaining pipe insulation
- switch the power to the solar controller on and ensure maximum storage vessel temperature selection is 60°C
- remove covers from solar collectors
- if installed, set the appropriate output temperature on thermostatic mixing valves in the hot water distribution pipes (this is an optional item)
- the system is now operational

Note: the system's pressure may increase or decrease during operation but this is normal. However, if at any time the system pressure shows zero bar, there is a fault.

repairs

Following installation, you may be unlucky and find a leak. With some small leaks, it may be possible to rectify quickly (for example: further tightening up of a compression joint using adjustable spanners).

There will be isolation valves in various places throughout the system so that different components or sections can be isolated without the need to fully drain the system. For instance, the pump already has isolating valves either side to allow it be removed if necessary.

However, it is often just as easy to completely drain the system and the commissioning procedure explains how to do this.

Before working on any component or section of the system, it is essential for safety reasons to ensure that:
- *the system is isolated from mains electricity*
- *the collectors are covered to avoid them heating up while you are working on them*

Leaks can be repaired quite easily with the aid of;
- PTFE sealing tape or hemp strands
- jointing compounds of a temperature and rating suitable for the fluid being carried (there are different requirements for pipes carrying antifreeze and domestic hot water)

The most likely point for a leak to occur is on a pipe joint.

If it is a soldered fitting then the fitting can sometimes be re-soldered without removal. Care should of course be taken if soldering indoors, especially in the roof space (be aware of roof timbers, storage boxes, dust and some insulation materials which may be flammable).

To attempt such a repair, all fluid within the pipe or fitting to be soldered must be completely drained, the outside surfaces cleaned with an abrasive pad or wire wool and a light coating of flux applied to the leaking joint.

Heat the area with a soldering blowtorch and feed a small amount of additional solder into the joint. Allow to cool, clean off excess flux and inspect before refilling and testing for leaks.

If re-soldering does not work, the faulty section will need to be cut out and replaced.

Compression joints may need to be re-sealed, which means taking the joint apart, cleaning it and re-applying one of the repair tapes, strands or compounds mentioned above.

Leaking threaded joints really need to be taken apart, cleaned up and re-sealed, possibly with new washers.

troubleshooting

If you experience a problem with this system design, use the table below to help identify the solution:

fault	comment
Pump doesn't run	a) check power is switched on/plugged in. b) isolate power supply and check wiring is correct from power supply to controller and pump. c) check controller settings. d) seized motor shaft; with power isolated, remove cover screw from centre of pump – a little water will come out. Behind the cover screw is another screw-head; rotate this with a screwdriver. Replace cover screw, switch on power and run pump.
Pump turns but flow regulator does not register a fluid flow / deliver hot water	a) valve closed in fluid circuit; check all valves and isolating points. b) NRV fitted wrong way round or seized; remove and check. c) air trapped in pump; Loosen pump cover screw. Air will bubble out. When bubbling stops, tighten cover screw.

d) air lock in system; release air from valves or by slightly loosening compression fittings at high points in pipes. Tighten fittings after and check for leaks.
e) air lock still in system; give it time - it often makes its own way to the air bleed point(s), where it can be released
f) debris trapped in circuit; check all parts of system where fluid aperture narrows (for example, just before NRV and flow regulator).

Error indicated on controller	a) consult controller manual.
Pump doesn't run when solar energy available	a) check temperature on/off variables are correct on controller (see RESOL manual). b) check sensors are correctly wired and there are no breaks in cabling (isolate power supply first). c) check Tmax value on controller is correctly adjusted. d) if storage vessel has already been heated to Tmax set temperature, pump will stop to protect system components (this is not a fault).
Noise when pump is running	a) check for air in pump; loosen pump cover screw. Air will bubble out. When bubbling stops, tighten cover screw. b) check pipes are well fixed and not vibrating against other surfaces.
Loss of fluid pressure	a) remove pipe insulation and check joints for leaks, repair as required and top up system with heating fluid to required pressure. Check that all components are adequately temperature rated or protected from system heat. b) check that fill and drain valve, air bleed point(s) and additional drain cock(s) are fully closed.

c) check for discharged fluid from the
   pressure relief valve; adjust expansion
   vessel gas precharge and refill system.
d) check membrane in expansion vessel has
   not ruptured; depress air valve and look for
   fluid release or decommission system,
   remove vessel, add air through valve and
   check for air leaks from fluid connection.
e) pressure gauge may be faulty; connect
   a temporary gauge to check, or
   replace pressure gauge.

how to get the best out of the system

To get the most out of a solar hot water system, there are some important
things to remember:
* don't switch the system off – the system is designed to collect, transfer
  and store solar energy to a hot water system without regular user
  intervention. Don't be tempted to switch the system off to conserve
  electricity (for example when on holiday or going away for the weekend).
* manage the energy contribution from the backup water heater – the
  gas/oil/wood boiler or electric immersion heater should be both time-
  and temperature-controlled. Set the timer to prevent the backup heater
  from contributing during daylight hours, and set the thermostat to limit
  the backup heater temperature contribution to 60°C maximum.
* to further improve the daily solar contribution, you may want to prevent
  the backup water heater from making a contribution until the evening.
  This is a particularly useful strategy to increase solar contribution during
  summer months.
* use hot water regularly – the system is designed to be 'demand driven'.
  The more hot water consumed, the more efficiently the system will run.
  If hot water is not used, the system will stop after providing a cylinder full
  of hot water as there is nowhere to store further solar energy.
* use hot water in late afternoon and early evening – this tends to be the
  most efficient time to consume hot water as it is immediately after water
  has been solar heated, and before the system has had time to lose very
  much of the stored heat.
* give the system a periodic health check – to ensure fluid pressure and
  flow are correct, the collectors are not damaged, pipe insulation is intact
  and controls are functioning as they should.

- the system fluid should also be checked periodically to ensure its chemical properties are intact (i.e. that it is still an antifreeze) and that the solution has not become acidic.
- an acidity check can easily be undertaken by extracting a sample of fluid and using litmus paper or a Ph testing kit, but the antifreeze check requires measuring the fluid density using a hydrometer or its refractive index using a refractometer. If these tools are not obtainable, a local solar heating engineer should be employed to undertake the periodic inspection of the entire system.

building a solar collector

There are numerous ways to make solar water heating devices. This chapter provides a practical guide to one way of making a solar collector that could be used in a fully-filled pressurised domestic solar hot water system, a design featured in LILI solar training courses and used throughout the UK.

This design is for a flat plate solar collector, made from readily sourced and relatively inexpensive materials. The exact dimensions are unimportant as the collector can be made any size to suit your needs. However, to get the most economical use of materials, it's worth building the collector sized to avoid wasteful off-cuts of material, particularly copper and aluminium components.

The copper piping is readily available in 2 or 3 metre lengths from all plumbing merchants and good DIY stores, and the aluminium in 1 metre lengths from the same outlets.

All measurements stated are approximate and can be altered to suit your own design or budget.

The pictures are based on a prototype that was built and tested and I'm sure it can be improved by altering the collector size and shape or thickness of wood used, etc.

collector casing and insulation

The casing provides protection to the absorber and pipes inside the collector and also helps to keep the rockwool insulation material dry. I chose to make the casing from treated wood, screwed together to form the four sides with a series of cross braces and a plywood backing sheet for rigidity. This particular collector was made in 'landscape' format but could also be made in portrait.

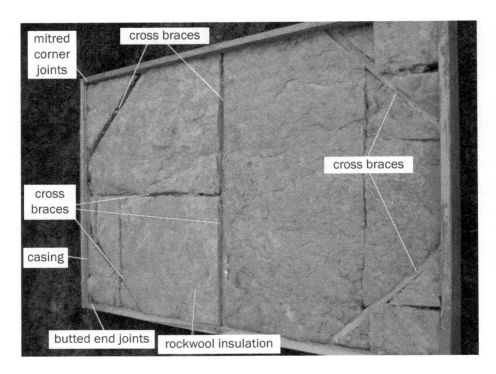

mitred corner joints

cross braces

cross braces

cross braces

casing

butted end joints

rockwool insulation

fig 155: collector casing and insulation

The timber used for the four sides was 22mm x 90mm treated ribbed planks in lengths to suit. These are sold as garden decking in DIY stores and the ribs in the planks are useful for air and drainage holes in the collector design but plain timber could be drilled as required if garden decking is too expensive. I did experiment with using the ribs as a runner to hold the glazing but this wasn't very successful.

The cross braces are made from 50mm x 25mm treated roof tile battens, cut to length as required. These are available from good DIY stores or roofing suppliers.

The timber sides are fixed as follows:
- the sides and cross braces are screwed together using 6 x 50mm wood screws (I use stainless steel screws)
- you can use mitre-type or butt-type joints at the corners of the casing (these pictures show mitre joints at the top corners and butt joints at the bottom corners)

- gaps in the top corner joints should be filled with exterior clear silicone sealant, but the bottom corner joints need air and drainage holes (provided by the ribs if using garden decking)

fig 156: mitred corner joint

The plywood backing sheet should be exterior grade (waterproof) and can be quite thin (less than 6mm is ideal as it is inexpensive and lightweight). The backing sheet can be nailed to the frame using 20mm long panel pins combined with a thin bead of silicone sealant. As an alternative to plywood, thin metal sheeting can be used if this is easier or cheaper to acquire.

The rockwool insulation is sold in DIY stores as rigid 'batts' and can be easily cut with a hardpoint wood saw to the size and shape required. I would recommend a depth of around 60-70mm (slightly more than the 50mm depth of the cross bracing).

fig 157: final positions for the pipes entering and leaving the casing

On one end of the casing (a side which will sit vertically once the collector is installed) two 22mm holes will eventually be drilled. The exact positions for these drilled holes are determined by the pipes inside the collector.

absorber

The absorber consists of a series of copper pipes meandering across the collector with aluminium plates attached.

The pipe configuration is quite flexible but the following pictures show the pipes entering and leaving the collector on the same side of the casing and meandering from bottom to top. This configuration makes it slightly easier to fit and remove the absorber from the casing during construction. For further information on pipe configurations within absorbers, please see the *solar collectors* chapter, page 33.

Whichever pipe configuration you choose, the fluid should take an equidistant path from entry to exit, so that the fluid cannot take a 'short cut'.

The pipes are 15mm diameter and joined using lead-free solder with end-feed solder fittings; these are all available from plumbing merchants or DIY stores.

fig 158: soldering pipes

The completed pipe configuration should be placed in the casing to ensure a good fit. Now you will need to drill the holes to pass pipes through the collector casing.

fig 159: pipe configuration

The gaps between each of the horizontal pipes should be equivalent to the measured width of the aluminium absorber plates, allowing for a slight overlap of plates where appropriate (see later in the instructions).

The next task is to paint the pipes. This should be done with high-temperature-resistant matt black paint. Paint for barbecues, available from DIY stores, is ideal for this.

Clean and roughen the surface of the pipes with wire wool or an abrasive pad.

It's best to apply at least two coats of paint allowing plenty of time between coats for the paint to dry and harden.

fig 160: paint the pipes

Next the absorber fins need to be cut to size. The absorber is made from 1 metre sections of heat-spreader plate; this is usually used in under floor heating.

The spreader plates have flat sections either side of a pressed channel designed to hold a 15mm pipe. On this prototype, I have experimented with cutting back the ends of the channel to try to hide sections of pipe and create a tidy appearance, though this isn't essential.

The spreader plates should be cut to length and laid out as a full absorber to check that they will fit together perfectly when finally assembled.

fig 161: preparing the spreader plates

Fig 161, clockwise from top left: measuring to trim back; cutting the channel with tin snips; folding back the cuts; arranging the trimmed plates into a full size absorber.

The upper surface of each of the spreader plates must now be cleaned and roughened with wire wool or an abrasive pad in order to help the paint adhere.

Before painting the spreader plates, take an unpainted length of copper tubing and push it into the pressed channel of each spreader plate. This is to check that the channel profile makes good all-round contact with the pipe and grips well. If this is not the case, remove the pipe, lightly nip the channel with water pump pliers and retest.

The upper surface of each spreader plate should be painted with one coat which should be allowed to dry and harden. The plates should now be ready to clip onto the pipe arrangement to form the full size absorber, and the absorber can be loosely inserted into the collector casing.

fig 162: preparing the spreader plates for painting

The absorber will need to be held in position. I use three screws, fixed through drilled holes where the absorber plates overlap into the wooden cross braces of the frame beneath.

fig 163: position the absorber

To accurately position these screws, pencil mark the casing at points where the cross bracing connects. Align a straight edge with the pencil marks and use a pen or screw to mark the point on this edge where the absorber plates overlap.

Check that this marked point does not coincide with hidden pipes underneath the absorber plates before drilling a hole in the absorber plate to accept a fixing screw, see fig 165.

pencil mark

fig 164 fix the absorber

Fig 164, clockwise from top left: marking cross braces on collector casing; marking overlap of plates along straight edge; screwing through plates to bracing; the three screw positions on the full size absorber.

Once the full-size absorber is fixed in position, a second coat of paint can be applied to cover any scratches.

Two strips of wood then need to be screwed to the inside of the collector casing, one on each side. The strips should fit 'flush' with the top edges of the collector casing, be between 15-20mm deep and are intended to provide an air gap between the absorber and the glazing.

fig 165: fitting wooden strips for air gaps

sensor position

A small off-cut of aluminium must be screwed to the absorber plate nearest the pipe exiting the top edge of the collector casing. This retaining strip will allow for a temperature sensor to be slipped through the hole in the collector casing and positioned alongside the pipe. If you are making more than one collector and all collectors will be mounted at the same angle and orientation, only the last collector in the array needs to have a temperature sensor retaining strip. This retaining strip must also be painted matt black.

fig 166: retaining strip for sensor

glazing and weatherproof trim

A sheet of 4mm, toughened British float glass can now be purchased which should be slightly smaller than the dimensions of the collector casing except on the bottom edge, where the glass will overhang the casing by 10-20mm, forming a drip edge.

Now that most of the screws have been fixed but before applying the glazing, it is a good idea to pressure test the pipe arrangement for leaks. At this point it is not too late to remove the pipes for repair if required.

A pressure test can be performed by either:

dry test: attach an air-pressure test gauge to one of the pipes exiting the collector casing and cap off any other pipe ends. Use a car foot-pump to raise the pressure through the shrader valve on the test gauge. Check that a pressure of 5 bar can be maintained over a period of one hour. The absorber must be out of sunlight for this test.

wet test: attach a water-pressure test gauge to one of the pipes exiting the collector casing and cap off any other pipe ends. Remove one of the caps and attach a garden hose pipe. Turn on the garden tap until the maximum pressure is achieved. Check that this pressure can be maintained over a period of one hour or, if no test gauge is available, leave the garden tap open and check visually for leaks every hour for four hours. The collector must be out of sunlight for this test.

Also, check that the temperature sensor slides smoothly through the hole in the wooden casing and beneath the small aluminium retaining strip; once the glazing is attached, this will be the only means of access. Widen the hole with a file if necessary.

To install the glazing, apply butyl-mastic tape 10mm wide to the uppermost surfaces of the collector casing, and then press the glazing firmly onto the tape. This tape is normally available from double glazing companies and adhesive or rubber suppliers.

fig 167: installing the glazing

Using spare spreader plates cut flat strips of aluminium to make into a weatherproof trim. The strips must be bent to slightly more than a right-angled profile (a straight piece of planed square edge 4" x 2" timber can be used to form the profile, and the slight over-bend can be finished by hand).

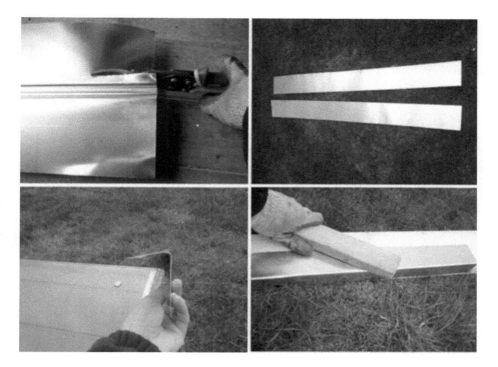

fig 168: *making the weatherproof trim*

When enough strips have been made to fit all around the uppermost edges of the collector casing, drill holes to accept fixing screws (these will be fixed to the *sides* of the collector casing, *not* to the top edges carrying the butyl-mastic tape).

A bead of clear silicone sealant should be applied to the upper edges of the glazing and the upper sides of the collector casing. Fix each weatherproof trim section in turn starting at the edge where the glazing overhangs. Press each section of trim down onto the bead of sealant and hammer a dozen or so panel pins through the aluminium and into the sides of the wooden casing.

A portion of trim should extend beyond the glass overhang. This can be cut back leaving a small piece of aluminium which can be bent around the glass overhang (helping to prevent the glass from sliding off the collector casing if the adhesive layers ever failed).

fig 169: fixing the weatherproof trim

Fig 169, clockwise from top left: drilling screw holes in weatherproof trim, beads of silicone sealant; trimming back the aluminium; weatherproof trim bent around glass overhang.

You may find that the weatherproof trim snags on the pipes sticking out of the casing. If so the aluminium should be cut to fit around the pipe holes.

fig 170: ensure the weatherproof trim fits around exiting pipes

Once all the sections of weatherproof trim are fixed, push the temperature sensor through the hole alongside the pipe and into position beneath the retaining strip.

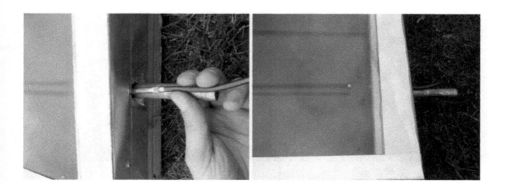

fig 171: positioning the temperature sensor

Seal the holes around the pipes with silicone sealant.

fig 172: the collector is essentially now ready to use

You'll find that there are some small scraps left over and some materials such as wood or copper pipe can be readily used when installing the rest of the solar hot water system.

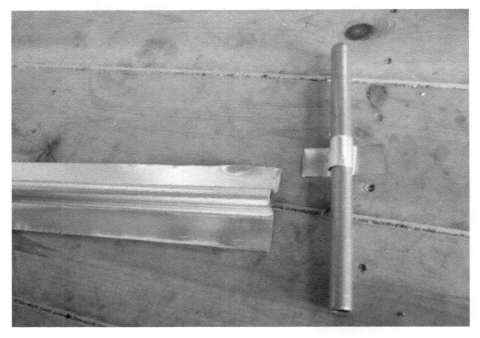

fig 173: use left over aluminium to make pipe clips

You may also wish to cut up the left over centre sections of aluminium spreader plate; they make reasonable pipe clips in conjunction with screws or nails!

As I've already mentioned, the exact dimensions of parts making up the collector are completely flexible. However, if you really want to make a collector the same as the one in the pictures, here are the dimensions of the parts making up the casing (all internal parts will of course have to be slightly smaller to fit inside).

glass:
- 1344mm x 920mm x 4mm, quantity = 1. Type: toughened, British float

wooden casing side sections:
- 910mm x 90mm x 22mm, quantity = 2. Type: treated and ribbed garden decking boards
- 1364mm x 90mm x 22mm, quantity = 1. Type: treated and ribbed garden decking boards
- 1320mm x 90mm x 22mm, quantity = 1. Type: treated and ribbed garden decking boards

casing backing:
- 1358mm x 906mm x 4mm, quantity = 1. Type: exterior or marine grade

other materials used:
- slicone sealant, quantity = 1 tube. Type: exterior grade, flexible and high temperature tolerant
- 50mm x 25mm wooden battens, quantity = approx 5 metres. Type: treated
- mineral wool insulation, quantity = approx 1.5 square metres x 60-70mm thick.
- 20mm Panel pins, quantity = approx 100
- 6 x 50mm wood screws, quantity = 50. Type: stainless steel
- glazing tape, quantity = approx 5 metres. Type: butyl-mastic 10mm
- spreader plates, quantity = approx 8. Type: aluminium 1000mm x 250mm
- 15mm copper pipe, quantity = approx 6.5 metres
- 15mm copper pipe fittings, quantity = 6. Type: female to female 90° end-feed elbow
- non-corrosive flux and lead-free solder for soldering
- matt black paint quantity = approx 400ml. Type: for barbecues or stoves
- temperature sensor, quantity = 1. Type: suitable for use with solar controller of choice

Good luck!

appendix a

cylinder volumes and dimensions

Height (millimetres) / Diameter (millimetres) not including insulation / Approximate Total Volume (Litres)

Height (mm) \ Diameter (mm)	300	350	375	400	450	500	600
600	38	48	54	60	73	88	123
700	45	57	64	72	89	107	151
750	48	62	70	78	96	117	165
800	51	66	75	84	104	127	179
900	58	76	86	96	120	146	206
1050	68	90	102	115	143	174	248
1100	72	95	107	121	151	184	262
1200	78	104	118	133	166	203	289
1300	85	113	128	145	182	223	317
1400	92	121	139	157	197	242	345
1500	99	132	151	169	212	261	373
1600	106	141	161	182	228	280	401
1700	112	150	171	194	244	299	428
1800	119	159	182	206	259	318	456
1900	126	169	192	218	274	337	484
2000	132	178	203	230	290	356	511

appendix b

expansion vessel sizing guide

system height in metres		2.5			5			10	
Number of collectors*	vessel nominal volume in litres	vessel gas precharge in BAR	HTM pressure in BAR	vessel nominal volume in litres	vessel gas precharge in BAR	HTM pressureq in BAR	vessel nominal volume in litres	vessel gas precharge in BAR	HTM pressure in BAR
1	18	0.8	1.2	18	1.0	1.4	24	1.5	1.9
2	24	0.8	1.2	24	1.0	1.4	35	1.5	1.9
3	35	0.8	1.2	35	1.0	1.4	50	1.5	1.9
4	35	0.8	1.2	35	1.0	1.4	50	1.5	1.9
5	50	0.8	1.2	50	1.0	1.4	80	1.5	1.9
6	50	0.8	1.2	50	1.0	1.4	80	1.5	1.9

*applies to ATLAS and WATT/Norfolk Solar flat plate collectors from the LILI range or flat plate collectors with a similar fluid capacity and stagnation temperature.

HTM: heat transfer medium (water / glycol)

system height: the distance between the highest and lowest parts of the solar installation

appendix c

shower water consumption and costs

Shower flow and cost estimates (water only; does not account for increased fuel to heat additional hot water)

	2 persons			3 persons			4 persons			5 persons		
	at 4L/M	at 7L/M	at 10L/M	at 4L/M	at 7L/M	at 10L/M	at 4L/M	at 7L/M	at 10L/M	at 4L/M	at 7L/M	at 10L/M
total consumed water volume in cubic metres	18.9	33.0	47.2	28.3	49.5	70.8	37.7	66.1	94.4	51.1	89.4	127.8
water charge per year	£21.76	£38.00	£54.35	£32.58	£56.99	£81.52	£43.40	£76.10	£108.69	£54.35	£95.10	£135.87
sewerage charge per year @ 90% water consumption	£21.18	£36.97	£52.88	£32.04	£55.46	£79.33	£42.24	£74.06	£105.77	£52.88	£92.55	£132.21
total charge for water and sewerage per year	£42.94	£74.97	£107.23	£64.62	£112.45	£160.85	£85.64	£150.16	£214.46	£107.23	£187.65	£268.08

Water charges (per cubic metre) in pence

year	2005	2006	2007	2008
water	89.42	102.43	106.46	115.14
sewerage	102.43	115.48	118.42	124.49

	% increase from previous year		
water	n/a	14.5	3.9	8.2
sewerage	n/a	12.7	2.5	5.1

assumptions:

each occupant takes one 7 minute duration shower per day

337 days per year consumption (28 days away)

2008 rates for water and sewerage charges from supplier

in East Anglia, UK

L/M = litres per minute total consumption (hot and cold mixed)

mains sewerage system; not septic tank or reed bed

appendix d

conversion tables

from		to	multiply by
DISTANCE / AREA			
yards	=	metres	0.914
metres	=	yards	1.094
feet	=	metres	0.305
metres	=	feet	3.281
inches	=	millimetres	25.4
millimetres	=	inches	0.039
square yards	=	square metres	0.836
square metres	=	square yards	1.196
WEIGHT / MASS / VOLUME			
pounds	=	kilograms	0.454
kilograms	=	pounds	2.205
gallons (UK)	=	litres	4.546
litres	=	gallons (UK)	0.22
gallons (US)	=	litres	3.785
litres	=	gallons (US)	0.264
FLOW RATE (VOLUME)			
litres per minute	=	gallons per minute (US)	0.264
gallons per minute (US)	=	litres per minute	3.785
PRESSURE			
BAR	=	pounds per square inch	14.503
pounds per square inch	=	BAR	0.068
kilopascals	=	pounds per square inch	0.145
pounds per square inch	=	kilopascals	6.894

TEMPERATURE

degree celsius	0	10	20	30	40	50	60	70	80	90	100
=											
degree fahrenheit	32	50	68	86	104	122	140	158	176	194	212

appendix e

periodic maintenance checklist

* use manufacturer's maintenance instructions instead where available

item	action
the system is leak-free	visual inspection of the fluid-carrying circuit
the expansion vessel gas precharge is acceptable (fully filled systems only)	where a fault is suspected, reduce fluid pressure to atmospheric and test gas precharge with air pressure gauge
system fluid pressure and flow rate are within acceptable limits	inspect pressure via gauge, inspect flow rate via sight glass on flow regulator
the collector casings and glazings are in reasonable condition and weathertight	visual inspection
the Heat Transfer Medium circuit is air-free during operation (fully filled systems only)	visual inspection via sight glass on flow regulator
valves are operational (air release, safety relief, non-return, motorised, solenoid)	twist test knob on safety valve and check valve discharges then reseats. Open and close air release valve(s), where a fault is suspected: remove and visually inspect non-return valves, electrically energise motorised and solenoid valves and visually confirm change of valve position via indicators
the Heat Transfer Medium circuit is not excessively noisy in operation	audible test with system running at all pump speeds
the pipe insulation condition is acceptable	visual inspection for Ultra Violet light degradation, rodent & bird attack, other physical damage or removal
any pressure devices discharge to a safe and noticable location	discharge small volume of fluid from safety relief valve and visually inspect route to discharge location
check collector roof fixings are sound, and roof penetrations are weathertight	visual inspection internally / externally
the electrical components have the correct settings and are functioning properly	inspect and test operation of light sensitive and thermostatic controls. Test activation of pump(s)
the system is correctly fused and there are no exposed electrical cables	visual inspection
the sensors are firmly and correctly positioned	visual inspection
the Heat Transfer Medium is sufficiently protected against frost damage	density check sample of Heat Transfer Medium using refractometer
the Heat Transfer Medium PH level is acceptable	check acidity / alkalinity of sample Heat Transfer Medium using litmus paper or PH solution test kit
back-up heat source control settings are acceptable	visual inspection of time and temperature controls of back-up water heater(s)
Blending valve(s) setting is acceptable	visual inspection and measure water temperature at outlet(s)

actual result	acceptable result	action taken
	leak free	
	consult manufacturer data	
	consult manufacturer data	
	no visible problems	
	no visible air bubbles	
	fully operational and do not leak when recommissioned	
	silent to low noise level; depending on design	
	majority intact / light damage	
	no leaks, no obstructions, discharge location is safe for users	
	no leaks, no structural corrosion of fixings	
	consult manufacturer data	
	no cable damage; sutiable earthing, suitable fuse rating and isolation	
	sensors cannot be easily removed from working position by accident / bird attack	
	frost protection below lowest expected winter night-time air temperature for location	
	PH 6.5 or above	
	consult manufacturer data	
	dependant on bacterial control measures vs. anti- scalding	

appendix f

hazards, risks and control measures

ACTIVITY	HAZARD	PEOPLE AFFECTED	POTENTIAL
assembling / moving access equipent	unstable access platform	installers, householders, public	high
	ladders striking overhead cables	installers	high
	weight of moving access equipment	installers	medium
working at height	person falling	installers, householders, public	high
	falling objects	installers, householders, public	high
general work on site	general construction hazards	installers, householders	medium
	hazardous fumes / particles	installers	low
	electric shock	installers	high
	bumps, cuts, etc	installers	medium
lifting collectors / equipment to roof	heavy / awkward lifting	installers	high
	collector dropped during lift	installers, householders, public	high
	dangerous wind gusts	installers	high
positioning and fixing collectors on roof	drill snatching	installers	high
	cuts from broken glazing	installers	medium
	burns from collector pipes	installers	high
soldering	burns	installers	medium
	fire	installers, householders	high
confined space work	hazardous fumes / particles	installers	high
	exposure to heat	installers	medium

LIKELIHOOD	RISK RATING	CONTROL MEASURES
low	medium	check equipment is level, set up correctly and adequately secured for the task
medium	medium / high	check for cables before moving ladders, find a safe route
low	medium / low	two people to move heavy access equipment
medium	medium / high	installers to be competent, use harnesses and edge protection where appropriate, restrict access below working area, only work in safe weather conditions
medium	medium / high	keep working platform tidy, restrict access below working area
medium	medium	keep working areas tidy, restrict access to working areas, use appropriate personal protective equipment (PPE), use suitable working platforms and don't overload
low	low	isolate or contain source, ensure ventilation, use PPE
low	medium	check for cables, isolate power where appropriate, use cordless tools or mains tools with RCD
low	medium / low	use sufficient lighting, check for protrusions, operatives to be competent, wear appropriate PPE
medium	medium / high	ensure operatives are competent, max lift weight 25kg per person, inspect condition of lifting equipment
medium	medium / high	restrict access below, use fall arrester where appropriate
low	medium	avoid lifting during wind gusts
medium	medium / high	good grip when drilling, secure and balanced working position, use torque limiting tools where appropriate
low	medium / low	handle glazed surfaces with care, wear suitable PPE
medium	medium / high	handle with care, use PPE, cover collectors from sunlight during install where possible
low	medium / low	operatives to be competent, use PPE
medium	medium / high	remove combustibles, operatives to be competent, use heat mats, fire extinguisher in working area, check area regularly after soldering
low	medium	good ventilation, usable means of escape, use PPE
low	medium / low	good ventilation, usable means of escape, regular breaks

resources

information

Department of Energy and Climate Change (DECC)

London
www.decc.gov.uk
0300 060 4000
Information on the Renewable Heat Incentive – financial incentives to install solar and other renewable heat technologies

Energy Saving Trust

London, Edinburgh, Belfast and Cardiff
www.energysavingtrust.org.uk
0800 512012
Administers the Renewable Heat Incentive

Euro Solar Thermal Industry Federation (ESTIF)

Brussels
www.estif.org
Maps of weather data for Europe and lots of information on the solar thermal industry

Health and Safety Executive

www.hse.gov.uk
Information leaflets and risk assessments on various relevant topics such as working at height

International Energy Agency (IEA)

www.iea.org
Task forces of experts in different aspects of solar energy carry out 5-year projects for the benefit of industry, and the world generally

LILI

www.lowimpact.org
01296 714184
See our solar hot water topic page for more information, books, links, twin- (and triple-) coil cylinders, solar hot water courses at various locations around the UK. Also, to discuss any issues raised in this book with the author, you can use the forum on LILI's website (under 'energy') www.lowimpact.org/forums

Norfolk Solar

www.norfolksolar.co.uk
01603 734851
The author's company – installing solar thermal in East Anglia

Met Office

www.metoffice.gov.uk
Lots of information on the UK weather and solar insolation

Plumbing: Heating and Gas Installations

R D Treloar, Wiley-Blackwell, 2006
Best plumbing book we've found, available from LILI

trade associations and competent persons schemes

Association of Plumbing & Heating Contractors (APHC)

Birmingham
www.competentpersonsscheme.co.uk
0121 711 5030
Established in 1925, a highly respected trade association for plumbing and heating professionals, it also operates one of the most wide-ranging competent persons schemes through which professionals can self-certify their work under the building regulations

CORGI

www.corgiservices.com
01256 548040
Basingstoke
Formerly the administrator of all authorised UK gas engineers but now a trade association and competent persons scheme provider

Department of Communities and Local Government

www.communities.gov.uk
Government department responsible for building regulations and
planning procedures in England and Wales

Microgeneration Certification Scheme (MCS)

London
www.microgenerationcertification.org
0207 090 1082
The organisation that sets out technical and operating standards for all
renewable and low carbon technologies and installers in the UK

Solar Trade Association (STA)

London
www.solar-trade.org.uk
0207 925 3575
The main trade association for solar energy professionals operating in
the UK

Logic Certification

Northolt, Middlesex
020 8839 2439
logiccertification.com
UKAS accredited training certification body that provides industry
recognized renewable energy training courses via a network of training
centers throughout the UK

other LILI publications

Learn how to heat your space and water using a renewable, carbon-neutral resource – wood.

This book includes everything you need to know, from planning your system, choosing, sizing, installing and making a stove, chainsaw use, basic forestry, health and safety, chimneys, pellet and woodchip stoves The second edition has been expanded to reflect improvements in wood-fuelled appliances and the author's own recent experience of installing and using an automatic biomass system.

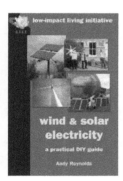

The author has been providing his own electricity from the sun and the wind for many years, and in this book he explains how you can do the same.

There are chapters on the various system components required (including inverters and charge controllers), how to put them all together, batteries, grid-connected systems, and there is even a basic electricity primer. Andy has analysed the output of his system for over 10 years, and these real-life figures are included.

The author grew up in Jamaica and was taught to make soaps by her grandmother. They grew all the plants they needed to scent and colour their soaps and even used wood ash from the stove to make caustic potash.

Her book is intended for beginners, includes both hot- and cold-process soap making, with careful step-by-step instructions, extensive bar, liquid and cream soap recipes, full details of equipment, a re-batching chapter plus information on the legislation and regulations for selling soap.

how to spin: just about anything *is a wide-ranging introduction to an ancient craft which has very contemporary applications. It tells you all you need to know about the available tools, from hand spindles to spinning wheels, what to do to start spinning, with illustrated, step-by-step instructions, and a comprehensive guide to the many fibres you can use to make beautiful yarns.*

Janet Renouf-Miller is a registered teacher with the Association of Weavers, Spinners and Dyers, and has taught at their renowned Summer School. She has also taught courses for many spinning and weaving Guilds, knitting groups, shops and voluntary organisations.

Lightning Source UK Ltd.
Milton Keynes UK
UKHW020819020119
334826UK00004B/263/P